Lettin' Go

UFO in the '80s & '90s

Martin Popoff

Lettin' Go

UFO in the '80s & '90s

Martin Popoff

WP
WYMER
PUBLISHING
Bedford, England

First published in 2019
by Wymer Publishing
Bedford, England
www.wymerpublishing.co.uk
Tel: 01234 326691
Wymer Publishing is a trading name of Wymer (UK) Ltd

ISBN 978-1-912782-08-6

Front & back cover images © Alan Perry

Printed and bound by
Clays Ltd, Bungay, Suffolk, England

A catalogue record for this book is available from the British Library.

Cover design by The Andys.

Contents

Preface   1

Chapter One: No Place to Run   5
  – *"Those years became known as the years of excess, didn't they?"*

Chapter Two: The Wild, the Willing and the Innocent   25
  – *""Shady characters always popping around the studio"*

Chapter Three: Mechanix   45
  – *"There's a pub in Switzerland better than the one we use in London"*

Chapter Four: Making Contact   71
  – *"If that's the way you feel, let's go right now!"*

Chapter Five: Misdemeanour   105
  – *"Chucking ideas about over cans of fine English ale"*

Chapter Six: Ain't Misbehavin'   121
  – *"The money started running out"*

Chapter Seven: High Stakes & Dangerous Men   127
  – *"I tried to keep the whole thing very straight and sober"*

Chapter Eight: Walk on Water   137
  – *"I have been happy in both worlds"*

Epilogue: 156
  – *"The last few years have been tough"*

Discography   159
Credits   162
About the Author   163
Martin Popoff Bibliography   164

Preface

G reetings, lovers of fine music. A little background is in order. I've been taking a number of my books that have been out of print and breaking them into early and later years books, many deserving two or even three volumes because of research I've done and interviews I've done since the books were last in print. I've worked through this now with Judas Priest and Black Sabbath—just the seventies so far, with *Judas Priest: Decade of Domination* and *Sabotage! Black Sabbath in the Seventies*—and here are the results of breaking my old 2005 book, *UFO: Shoot Out the Lights* into two action-packed volumes.

So, what you're looking at here is the follow-up to *Lights Out: Surviving the '70s with UFO*, which covered quite tidily 1969 to 1979, comprising the Mick Bolton era of the band and the original Michael Schenker era of the band.

The present volume, I gotta tell you, one of the most hotly debated topics in the UFO community, is how much the Paul "Tonka" Chapman era of the band gets short shrift. And yes, you can count me in the controversial camp that picks Paul over Michael. Or, well, not really. I prefer Michael as an artist, but I prefer the songs on the albums with Paul, and really, that's down to both Paul and Neil Carter, essentially at the music end. So yes, pretty much my heart tells me that my three favourite UFO albums, in order, are *No Place to Run*, *The Wild, the Willing and the Innocent* plus *Mechanix*. Now, sure, it gets a little filmy with *Mechanix*, because on any given day I could put the likes of *No Heavy Petting* or *Obsession* over that one, but you get the point. Actually, it's kind of shocking to me how much I like *Mechanix* now, because back in the day, I thought it was goofy. Still, there is a warmth there that is missing from the seventies output, and that's really what it all comes down to for me in old age: which of these records keep me happy?

This is why it was such a joy doing this book, because what you find in the following pages is the most detailed and reverent examination of the first three UFO albums of the eighties that has ever been committed to print thus far. And then, of course, it's on and on into the twilight years, where, frankly, the music ain't so hot. But then there's the return of Michael Schenker for *Walk on Water*, and that record... many, many UFO fans think that one is just peachy, as do I.

So again, I'm always quite surprised about the heated debate between which version of UFO is better, the Michael Schenker era or the Paul Chapman era. I mean, obviously, the huge consensus is that the band's golden era was the latter half of the seventies with Michael, and in fact it's always a little disconcerting to see that many of those who believe that, completely dismiss the Paul Chapman albums. But we Paul Chapman plumpers, we seem to be open-minded enough to love the Schenker albums as well. What gives there?

Anyway, more about process, what you're going to realise in the following pages is that this current volume is set up similar to the *Lights Out* book, which was pretty much an examination of the albums, track by track, production, playing, lyrics, album covers, just bam, bam, bam and onto the next album, demarcated because each project gets a chapter, pure and simple. This is what I care about: the albums. Hope you do too.

One other note, for those of you who managed to get a copy of my *Shoot Out the Lights* book, I think you'll be pleasantly surprised at the wealth of new information that has been added to this volume, and much of it through new primary interviews I've done with the likes of Andy Parker, Paul Chapman, Paul Gray, Nick Tauber, Kit Woolven, Laurence Archer, along with additional interviews with the expected suspects, Michael Schenker, Phil Mogg and Paul Raymond (I don't think I've had another personal chat with Pete Way since, but oh well).

By the way, something pop fruity I should mention, I've taken a few side trips here and there, because I wanted to make sure I gave justice to a few great UFO "family" albums, most pointedly MSG's *Assault Attack* and Mogg/Way's *Chocolate Box* album, which I dare say is a bona fide UFO classic, just not given the band name UFO. Seriously, that record smokes, and I wanted to give it some vastly overdue attention.

I also touched down here and there on the career of Waysted. I often have to remind myself, when I grouse that Paul Chapman hasn't done much since UFO, that he spearheaded what is really one of my favourite bands that I keep forgetting about—the great Waysted, and so that band gets mention as well. And by the way, also when I get down on Paul for his output, I have to remind myself that he made those two cool Lone Star albums back in the seventies (you can get my mini stories of those as eBooks from zunior.com). And yeah, just in general, I do keep an eye on what Michael is doing as UFO stumbled past 1983 and into the weeds.

So that's it. We'll keep this short. I would've liked to keep things extra tidy and made strictly a book looking at the 1980s, but that would really be stretching your patience with my whole "slow food" approach I'm taking with some of my favourite bands. So please accept that I've gone beyond the eighties, which has, as a by-product, resulted in a little bit of an unwieldy title for this book, but there you go.

Anyway, on with the action. To reiterate, my biggest joy with this book was the idea that I could proselytize at length for the Paul Chapman records and that I most definitely get to do. So... er, thanks!

Martin Popoff
martinp@inforamp.net, martinpopoff.com

Chapter One
No Place to Run

*"Those years became known as
the years of excess, didn't they?"*

A fter a hat trick of records—*Lights Out*, *Obsession* and *Strangers in the Night*—in both the American and UK charts, UFO found themselves without their golden egg. That golden egg, golden god Michael Schenker, was now gone, with the inevitable brought in as replacement. As discussed in book one of our saga, *Lights Out: Surviving the 70s with UFO*, Paul "Tonka" Chapman had worked with the band post-*Phenomenon* and pre-*Force It*, also leading up to this record with live dates in support of the band's 1979 double-live album *Strangers In The Night*, if you buy the fact that an "in concert" album can have a tour. Chapman's main claim to fame however thus far was his work on two Lone Star albums, the '76 self-titled debut and *Firing on All Six* the following year, the latter featuring singer John Sloman who would later join Uriah Heep, another British institution going through growing pains in 1979.

"There were always different people considered, but nothing really went anywhere with anybody else," says UFO vocalist Phil Mogg, on adopting Chapman into the ranks. "We were always a bit of an insular band. It was kind of the people you grew up with and the people you played with. It was even a bit of a wrench when Andy (Parker) left. We were always one of those bands, where it's better the devil you know. I don't think it's a great idea anyway to get somebody who is predominantly known. When Michael left and we got Paul Chapman in, we could have gone out and got some antsy fancy name, but it was better to have somebody in the band who was going to be a band mate, a band player, somebody you knew. Michael is more insular and Paul's an extrovert, so it was from one extreme to another. In terms of tension, no, that was later, in the mid eighties. Those years became known as the years of excess, didn't they? Not success, excess. I think we did our fair share of that course."

"A bit difficult with Paul," notes keyboard man and second banana guitarist Paul Raymond, years later summing up his relationship with Chapman. "Very different sort of character. He's not as dedicated to his practice and his music as Michael."

But Chapman was indestructible; hence the aforementioned nickname "Tonka." "Well, that goes back around the eighties, when the heroin thing started, and the drink thing," says Paul, elaborating on the etymology. "It was always a drink thing, but in Lone Star, and even in early UFO, it was always… everyone smoked dope; it was what you did. It was like, when everybody else would be so passed-out, the only one that doesn't have a driving licence is me and I would be the one that had to drive across Scandinavia, this kind of thing. And I'd have to be the one that checked us into the hotel or got the boat tickets to get the band on the boat."

"And Phil started saying, 'He's indestructible. He's like one of those things that you wind up. What do you call them toys?' Somebody said 'Tonka toys!' 'Yeah,' he said, 'that's it.' So we were coming back down the M1, I'm driving the Range Rover and he's in the back throwing up or something like that, and he's supposed to be driving. And he's like, 'Well done, Tonka!' And I think Ross or Gary Bushell was there or somebody and it ended up in print and from then on it just kind of stuck. And in the end, you bump into people like Joe Elliott, 'Hey Tonka, how's it going?' It wasn't even Paul anymore. So it was the indestructible thing. Well, that's how it was then. It's not like that anymore. You get old and you calm down a bit."

And where was the now-exiled Mr. Schenker while Paul was on board burning up stages in support of *Strangers in the Night*? Well, he rejoined his brother Rudolf in Scorpions for that band's 1979 scorcher *Lovedrive*.

"What happened was that I had just left UFO," explains Michael, on the strange turn of events. "My brother heard about it. The Scorpions were just bringing in a new guitarist. My brother wanted me to play on parts of the new album. He gave me a tape and I went into the studio and played it. It went down so well that they asked me to join. I was already worn-out but because it was my brother, I decided to forget about all those things. Also, I forgot that if I were to play live with them then they would play a whole lot of songs from records they made before *Lovedrive*. I was going to have to copy all of those songs. I felt like, 'What am I doing here?' I was copying and playing Uli Roth's stuff. I like to keep the highlights and improvise the rest. I could not do that. I found myself in an unhappy place."

"I was afraid of touring," continues Schenker. "When *Lights Out* made it into the charts, I got so scared that I would have to constantly tour that I just sold everything and went away. So, it goes without saying that what happened with the Scorpions was a similar situation. I had very bad stage fright. I was taking prescription tablets so that I could go onstage. I was taking them before I went on instead of drinking, but then I started taking the tablets and drinking together. It was too much of an effort and too much of a nuisance."

"I asked myself, 'what am I doing here? Why have I chosen this profession?' God has his own way of making you strong. I think there was a reason why I had to go that way. What you are most afraid of comes right at you. I learned the hard way to lose my shyness and I grew out of it. I could not even make interviews back then. I remember one time they switched a tape on and the guy left the room and left me sitting there with the tape on. I was only 18. Phil was next door and he wondered why he didn't hear anything. I was just looking at the tape rolling. The guy comes back and says, 'How did it go?' I was like, 'How did what go?' He couldn't understand why I didn't say anything. Most people have a lot to say, even when they are not asked. He thought I was like that, but I was not. I would only say something when someone asked me a question. I would never talk."

"I missed out on ten years of social skills because I was too busy being creative," continues Schenker. "I was like a big movie star who was always working and missed out on his son's first baby steps. I had no idea how to be social or how to behave. Most of what I have learned about being social I have learned since I have been in the United States. I moved here in 1989. I have been to a lot of self-improvement programs. I am much happier now that I'm not so shy. Life is more fun and flows much easier. I think that is why my guitar playing is flowing better. I used to play so tense that it would slow me down. I would try so hard and I was actually getting slower. I would hit the string harder than I would need to and I would press down harder than I would need to. I would be worn out after two solos."

When asked whether his brother was angry when Michael quit the band, Schenker says that "it hurt him. "He probably thought I was playing with him or being an egotistical person. People didn't understand what I was suffering from. I knew that if I told them, 'I can't do this. Please get Matthias Jabs back. I have to leave,' that they would have talked me into staying. I was easily manipulated. I was always the youngest member in the band by six or eight years; I would just follow the pack. They didn't understand that I suffered from panic attacks. I started having them when I was 15 years old. They didn't really understand what my health condition was and where I was in my head. I think it hurt them a lot but I don't think they ever really understood the truth about the whole thing."

Fact is, UFO not only didn't understand, they took the piss out of Michael relentlessly, aggressively cutting him up in a language he barely understood. That right there is considered by most followers of the band to be the main reason Michael broke down psychologically, putting him in a debilitating state that he didn't climb out of, essentially, arguably, until some time well into the 2000s.

Offering a bit of detail on the transition from Michael to Paul, drummer since the beginning, Andy Parker, explained to Metal-Rules that, "Paul was in the band first as a second guitar player. After we recorded *Phenomenon* and Michael had "Doctor, Doctor," with the double lead guitar, we had to take that on the road. He said it was going to be difficult for him to do it, so maybe we would have to think about getting another guitar player to play the rhythm and the extra lead."

"So we did auditions and we got Paul Chapman. As it turned out, it didn't work out very well, because it was like putting two cooks into one kitchen—it was a bit too much. It didn't really work to have two guitar players at the same time all the time because Michael's style is so... you know, when you've got two really good lead guitar players, it was like those fucking solos... it was actually quite exciting, but it didn't work because Michael's the lead player on the albums, so the solos were all Michael's. It's difficult to ask someone who can play really well solo-wise to just play rhythm, you know?"

"After that we went back to a four-piece and then decided that maybe a keyboard player would be better," says Andy. "That's when we got Danny Peyronel and did *No Heavy Petting*. Danny was great, but he had more of an ego of a solo kind of guy, so that's when we got Paul Raymond and Paul worked perfectly. He's so underrated, the guy sings, he plays guitar, he plays keyboards, he's just great. The line-up with Phil, Pete, Michael, Paul and me, I think was just a great line-up. Paul Chapman came in again when Michael disappeared overnight, because we knew him. Paul did that American tour for us, for which we were all very grateful. Then of course Michael came back and did the *Strangers in the Night* album. He said he'd come in and do the live album and then he'd be gone. The last part of the tour was the British tour and then Michael left. Paul came back in and we did some great albums."

The record that the now Schenker-less, but still familiar UFO would come up to begin the new decade with was to be called *No Place to Run*, and, despite the loss of Schenker, the album turns out to be one of the finest in the UFO canon—certainly this writer's favourite of the whole lot.

A couple of exotic things happened to the band at this point. Number one, the tropical locale of Montserrat had been chosen for recording (the now legendary Air Studios had just opened for business in '79 and UFO were arriving in early summer). Number two was that none other than fifth Beatle George Martin had been put in charge of said recording, a logical choice given that the Montserrat studio was an extension of Martin's vision, namely his London location of the same name, established in 1969. Fact was however, the band's first choice to produce was Ted Templeman, hot with Van Halen. But Templeman was a Warner Bros. staffer and could only do one outside project a year. That, coupled with the band's visa problems in the States had the guys looking elsewhere. George Martin had been having trouble convincing bands to make the trip to Montserrat, and so with UFO he had said, look, if you record there, I'll produce it.

"*No Place to Run* was weird," recalls a bemused Phil Mogg, looking back. "It was interesting because we had George Martin there. It was an odd combination and we did it at Montserrat, which made it even more illogical for a rock album. But George was tremendously nice (laughs). Which was... you know, we'd worked with quite a few assholes before, quite a few people who were kind of... there was no tension with George and he was extremely nice, very helpful. You could not, *not* get on well with him; it was just great working with him. And his engineer was excellent too."

Adds Phil with typical dry wit, "That was when Michael had gone off, and his last words were, 'Poor, poor, poor "Rock Bottom."' That was it. From the studio he left, and we never saw him again. So yes, Paul came in, and Chrysalis had this whiz idea of getting George Martin to do the album, which we thought was really odd. But then we thought, 'Oh, this will be good; we can get some great string arrangements out of this.' And then George had been briefed to do a rock album. So we were at odds there. And then we went to Montserrat to do it, which the record company said, 'Oh, would you like to go to Air Studios in Montserrat?' And we went, 'Oh, yeah, fantastic!' And I just remember it being a very different album, being in Montserrat, sunshine, in the Caribbean, working with George, which was great."

"He was a great guy, really relaxed, really laid-back," recalls drummer since the very beginning, Andy Parker. "I mean, UFO was a completely different kind of thing for him. You know, the way we work, he was used to... in fact, he even said this. He said, well, I'm kind of used to John and Paul coming in with their acoustic guitars and playing me the song. Well, with us, he didn't get that, because there's no lyrics written and there's no melodies or anything until, pretty much, the backing tracks are done. So that was different for him."

"But he just has great ideas about stuff, about how to make things sound a little different, or just a different spin on it you wouldn't normally get. Having come from Ron Nevison to him, you know, very different backgrounds. Nevo was all kind of rock, but George had done everything. And he was really easy to work with, really laid-back. And of course, God, he's the Beatles producer, so you're a little bit nervous. And Geoff Emerick was an absolute pleasure, because even by the time we were recording with George, 1980, his hearing was suffering then, so Geoff was really his ears. But George was all about arrangements and ideas, and there's some great stuff on that album. I don't know about you, but I still think to this day that those albums don't get the attention they should've got."

"But no, George was fabulous, although I just think he wasn't prepared," laughs Parker. "At least for a band like us, which is odd to say. He made that comment to us about John and Paul bringing in their acoustic guitars and playing the songs. We never really had finished songs until we hit the studio. We were sort of unprepared. Phil would have lyrics, or lyric ideas, the guys would have riffs, maybe put those words with that riff, and that bit with that bit, you know what I'm saying? So it was a lot more work. George never worked that way. He was used to guys coming around saying, 'Here's your song. Two guitars and riff and here you go.' So it was a bit of a struggle for him."

"Plus the band at that time was managerially in turmoil. We had this manager that had caused us a lot of grief. But George was fabulous and really made the best out of us. There we were on this island miles from anywhere, kind of rough and ready too. The power would go out every day and it was kind of odd. We've never experienced that sort of thing and he and Geoff Emerick were just brilliant; they did a fabulous job. That album, out of any of the Chapman albums, is one of my favourites because a) I got to work with George Martin, and b) he really did pull it together."

"Amazingly fit," continues Andy. "I don't know how old he was when he did that album, but he swam miles. There was one white sand beach on the island. Most of them were black because it had been a volcanic island. But there was this white sand beach and you can only get there by boat. So one day George was going to do some mixing, some bits and pieces, so we said we'll go to this beach. They took us in this boat, dropped us off, on the beach, and then Geoff took the boat back and dropped George at the beach where you could drive to. Because it was a long, long way."

"And they came back with the boat, and I think about two hours later, we suddenly see George walking up the beach out of the water. Because Geoff had dropped us off and gone, and George was going to get in the car, but he didn't have his car keys and he swam from two miles or so away, 'round this head. So he swam back! And I was just blown away. Because we were young and he was a lot older than us and he wasn't even panting! My God. If you've ever been in the sea, you know, 100 yards, well, that will do. But he was great. And Geoff Emerick was a real gentleman. It was a wholly different experience, having come from Gary Lyons and Ron Nevison."

"They've got those little tin hut bars, haven't they?" queries Phil, when asked about extracurricular activities so far from home. "The ones by the side of the road, and mainly you would go down to the beach, and then you would come up and do some recording. Of course, we'd been used to recording in towns and it was just very odd recording in that environment. In actual fact, it makes you feel like not working much. Fortunately we had quite a bit of the material done, but it's funny singing what you would consider to be city songs on a Caribbean island. It was a bit odd. If we had been there before and done some writing there, the songs might have come out a bit different. I particularly liked that at 6:00 they'd break off for G & Ts on the veranda overlooking the swimming pool and down the valley to the sea. And you're going, 'Wow, this is really something.'"

"Oh, we did some pictures there for Hipgnosis too," continues Mogg. "They have those. One of them was one of those ones where you're at the bottom of the pool reading a newspaper and stuff. They never really saw the light of day. See, the original cover was done in King's Cross, London. That used to be a taxi gas station that was open all night. But that's gone now."

"It's a very alien, very hostile environment," explains Paul Raymond, adding his view of the tropical paradise. "That studio actually doesn't exist anymore, does it? I think it got blown away in a hurricane (ed. Hurricane Hugo, 1989—a new location in Lyndhurst Hall, London was unveiled in '91). The weather sort of takes over at times, and after dark, just about every creature known to man, that you don't want to see, comes out (laughs). It's a funky place."

I asked Paul Chapman if George had ever done anything even remotely as heavy as UFO before hooking up with the boys. "Nothing really. He did the Cheap Trick thing right after us, but that's not really heavy. To be honest, I think he had just come straight off America or something like that." Indeed Martin had worked with America on their '79 album *Silent Letter*, and would move on to a Beatle-esque band of a different sort in Cheap Trick for their highly under-rated *All Shook Up* opus.

No Place to Run opens with a dramatic drone called "Alpha Centauri," the first piece Paul Raymond cites when asked about fresh ideas Martin brought to the table. "He did a couple of little Beatles tricks. There's a thing in 'Alpha Centauri' which sounds like a kick drum, but it doesn't actually sound like a kick drum. It's kind of like a heartbeat sound. And actually what it is, is a plastic piano stool hit with a drumstick, with a lot of low EQ on it. But it's a sound that you couldn't identify what the sound was. He goes, 'I think we'll try this.' 'Is he mad?!'"

"But then you realise what he's done with The Beatles, the hours he spent in the studio making sounds. But yeah, that was a keen idea. He's a very clever man... speeding things up and slowing them down; there were a lot of weird noises and synthesizer noises that weren't actually synthesizer. He's a very clever man, but he never gives away any secrets. You know, as much as I tried to get some of the Beatles things: 'How did you do that thing on that George Harrison song?' And he went, 'Oh, is that the time? I have to be going!' (laughs). He'd always change the subject."

"Alpha Centauri," all 1:57 of it, fades out to give rise to one of the most heroic sounding UFO rockers ever tracked. "Lettin' Go" cruises and grooves on a timeless hard rock riff, somewhat like a British take on Aerosmith, especially come chorus time, which, incredibly, takes the song even higher.

"The lyrics, 'I don't think I can last,' something like that," laughs Phil. "We were all burnt out; we had toured, toured, toured, and then recorded, recorded, and then toured and recorded. I think we were all getting pretty whacked by that point, so 'Lettin' Go' had to do with that." Still, Phil's lament is kept general enough to be about anybody caught in the trudge of structured, predictable work.

"That one was great to play live," recalls Paul Chapman. "The intro, 'Alpha Centauri,' and the outro I remember came out pretty neat. The intro is two backwards double-tracked guitars, the way it sort of sucks itself in. If you ever try to do that you have to turn the tape over and start at the end of the song. Plus the ending, with those little chime guitars? The ones that sound like little Christmas guitars? Those were kind of backwards reverb, but I suppressed the 12th fret and sort of tapped it all out. I never actually played it with my left hand. So you get these delays, echoes. I thought it was perfect; it added delicately to something that was kind of steamy and heavy."

"Very eye-opening from a technical point of view," adds Chapman, adding further to our profile of George Martin. "Very creative, it's like the days when studios were studios and nothing was digital of course—hardly anyway—maybe the odd harmonizer here and there. When rock began, to make a record you had to create things. You had to use an idea that nobody had ever used and when it comes out you'd go, 'Holy shit that sounds fantastic; I should patent that idea.' And George was the same way. George was very upper, upper class conservative. 'Oh, it's 6:00; I think it's time for my gin and tonic. Fetch the bottle, please;' this kind of approach. And he would go 'Fuck' or 'Fuck the grammar' and everybody would gasp."

"But technically he was incredible. I saw him do things where you would say 'How the hell did you do that?!' You're trying to find a pitch on a harmonizer and he'd say to Geoff Emerick, who was in the studio, 'Play me an A on that piano.' So he goes and plays an A, and he would go 'Okay, that's the note that Phil is hitting here and we want a third above it,' a major interval, which is a musical interval; it's a space between two notes. And Phil would say, 'That's too high; I can't do it.' And Geoff came in and he had a watch with a calculator, and he said, 'Okay, set that harmonizer at 98.73,' and Geoff goes over and punches it in and he says to Phil, 'Now sing it into the microphone.' And Phil goes up and hits an A and all of a sudden a note comes out which is a perfect major third above it. And I said, 'How the hell did you do that?!' And he said, 'It's very simple Paul; it's all in the log.' He went into this huge explanation about frequencies and divisible numbers of notes. I said, 'Show me that! I have to know how to do that; that's incredible!' He said, 'Oh, it's all in my book on page such and such' and he gave me a copy of his book and signed it. I must have read that page a thousand times and got a harmonizer and tried doing it with the calculator and it just wasn't working and I must have sat there for ten hours."

"And he's musically trained from a classical standpoint," continues Tonka. "You start out and you're just in awe because this guy is fantastic and he's done all the Beatles stuff, but after about a month in the studio, things mellow out and he's just a regular guy. When everybody left Montserrat, I was the last person there before we went back and that's when we did 'Alpha Centauri.' The original idea, why we left it until the end... all I wanted to do was make a 'play-on.' All I wanted to do was write a piece of music for the play-on tape before the band came on live."

"When we did the previous tour, we were using one that Michael did on his Revox. I said, 'Look, it sounds really shitty. The playing is okay but it sounds really bad going over a PA system in an arena. It's a two-track machine. I want to do one full-blown, the whole bit.' So George was like, 'Hey, let's put the synthesizer on there and speed it up!' I said we need a bass drum like a heart and he said bang the piano stool and put a towel around your hand and we just kind of farted around for three days and that's how we did it. And once we had done it, I said it's too good to use just as a live intro. So when we shipped all the tapes back to London and everybody listened to it, they said, 'Oh, that's got to be the opening of the album.' So it was nice working with him from a creative point of view."

But into the first track proper, one suddenly notices the record's huge drums, "Lettin' Go" rolling large, start to finish. "George was less invasive," reflects Andy. "Ron Nevison used to get really into wanting to tune the drums himself, and put heads on that he likes and stuff, to the point where sometimes it became where I couldn't really play it, not to the point that I liked. He made the kit very alien to me. I mean, he did get a good sound, but we used to bang heads a lot over that. He wouldn't like what he was getting. So he would put this head on there and say 'I'm going to tighten the kit right up.' And it's like, well, maybe that's not how I play. That doesn't feel right to me."

Asked if his drums tracks were all recorded at Montserrat, Andy answers, "I thought *all* the recording was done at Montserrat. At least all my recording was done at Montserrat, absolutely. There may have been some overdubs done at Air London, but all my stuff was definitely done at Montserrat, all the drums, bass, yeah. I went back to California and the guys went back to England, I think, after that. The other guys. They'd moved back to England so maybe there was some stuff done there. But they had done most of it, as far as I know, in Montserrat, which now doesn't exist—it's completely gone."

Next up was an explosive metalized cover of old blues chestnut "Mystery Train." "That was kind of a strange one," notes Raymond, on the Little Junior's Blue Flames hit, writing of the track credited on the UFO album to both Junior Parker and Sam Phillips, although it's Parker alone on the original from 1953. "We thought that might be a good song to do, and actually, a guy from the record company played the song down the telephone, so we could listen to it. We couldn't go to a record store and buy it, so we sort of listened to it down the phone. I don't think it was even faxed. I think he had to telex the words. This song was going back a long time ago. No one could quite remember how it went."

"Because I love Elvis; I used to play it when I was the kid," says Chapman on the choice of "Mystery Train" as an adequate cover, adding his version of the long distance runaround. "It was an idea I had for a while. The funny thing about that is we were in Montserrat, and if you remember, Montserrat is an island 17 miles long and nine miles wide; it's tiny. They have like eight telephones on Montserrat and about six cars. It's pretty third world. And they've got this high-tech studio right in the middle of it, or they used to have. Anyway, cast your ballot, "Mystery Train" was the one that came out. I knew how the song went but not all the words. But we didn't have a copy. So we called Chrysalis over phone No.21 or something like that and they dug up from somewhere a copy of "Mystery Train" and they played it to us over the phone from the office in London, and we recorded it on the two-track, on the two-inch. We hooked the phone up to the machine and put it into like track number one and we EQed the whole thing, and it sounded great, believe it or not. Imagine: we learned it from the version through the phone wire from London to Montserrat."

"Yeah, I've always been attracted to songs about trains," is Phil's two cents on the track. "There are quite a few train fanciers in the band. So "Mystery Train" we had played live before and we just had the urge to do it on the album."

Paul goes on to explain how UFO would interact, how they would write and record together. "That would alter. See, when you get together and you've comes straight off the road... I put down a lot of ideas on the road. At the time you didn't have portable four-tracks. But I would always take something that was the best recordable system at the time and I'd be back at the hotel or at sound checks or anywhere, tuning rooms before gigs. Some days I would purposely go down to the gig early if I got a creative urge and I'd put things down whether it be on bass or guitar or both if I could do it, and then I would play them for Phil when we came off the road and say, 'This is my stable of ideas; this is what I have from the last year.' He would go 'Well, that one is really good, that one is really good, I can hear things over that one,' and then I would say, 'Let me put these on a tape for you and you take them home.' And then I would work on some new stuff or start juicing up some of the old ones... 'This one fits with that, let me change the key on this, these two fit together,' this kind of thing. And I'd say 'Phil, come on over and let me play something.'"

"When we were at home we had more of an elaborate set-up, four-track reel-to-reels, little mixers. The equivalent of the home studio these days was really quite primitive back then. So we would work back and forth. I would say, 'Give me what you have with your idea on it' and we would bounce it back again, maybe add a bridge, and now I'm working with it again with the vocal idea in my head. And I would put a bridge to it and he would say, 'Okay, why don't we move that part over there?' And that's how 'Lettin' Go' came together. It was a good writing system. In other situations, if Phil was drawing a blank, we would go and record the whole thing and Phil would be up in his room with the backing track as we recorded the next one. While we were doing one, Phil would be up there with one of the previous ones and then I would be going up, or Pete would be going up, and monitoring the situation."

Track four on side one of *No Place to Run*, "This Fire Burns Tonight," is a relaxed, melodic hard rocker that adds proudly to the band's cache of such radio-potential songs, the lyric telling the melancholy story of a band on the road, driving all night, similar in nocturnal self-reflection to Bob Seger's "Turn the Page." Turns out this track is an example of a song that came from Paul's previous band Lone Star, who had just been working on a third album, these demo sessions remaining unreleased for years, until seeing light in 2000 on Zoom Club, as *Riding High: The Unreleased Third Album*.

Paul explains: "The funny thing is, when we were doing the third Lone Star album, I took it with me into UFO. And a lot of that became *No Place to Run*. Like for example, 'This Fire Burns Tonight' was a complete Lone Star song with different lyrics. If you look at *Riding High* and you listen to the song 'Travelling Man,' it's exactly the same song, everything, right down to the bridges, the intros, only with John Sloman singing instead of Phil. Phil would never ever sing anybody else's lyrics, unless we were doing a cover, like 'Mystery Train.' But of all this stuff I brought into the band, I'd already written the lyrics, but he wanted to redo them. Phil would not sing my words (laughs). You know, fair enough. But playing with Pete and Andy, these songs took on a new life."

Side one of the original vinyl closes with a gorgeous, yearning ballad called "Gone in the Night." Paul Raymond offers some lovely piano before the chorus turns dark with howling guitars. It is, arguably, one of the greatest ballads of UFO's career. The 2009 remastered reissue of the album contains what is purported to be an "alternative studio version" of the song. If it's different, this writer can't hear it, however it seems that the solo section to wind out the song might go on for another 15 seconds or so. It is also slightly less hi-fidelity, so perhaps it's the same recording but not remastered. Also included, however, are punchy and powerful live renditions of "Lettin' Go," "Mystery Train" and "No Place to Run," from the Marquee, November 16, 1980.

Side two opens with the type of UFO song that could only come from Pete Way, a man without a plan who nonetheless delivers "three chords and the truth," in this case, a song with time-honoured chord structures, namely yet another of the seemingly infinite variations on "Louie Louie" one can wring from the ether if the attitude is right and the antennae are up.

Not to Tonka's taste evidently. "Actually, 'Youngblood' was one of my least favourite on that album. I can remember when I was listening to the first mix of it and I looked at Andy Parker and I said, 'Is that it?! Everything sounded so dry. Is that it?!' And George was going, 'It sounds fine to me!' And I was going, 'Well it doesn't sound fine to me.' Although you can't actually come out and say that to George Martin. You have to be a little more diplomatic about it. But live, that was one of my favourite songs. It was like ten times heavier, a really cool live song."

Reflects Andy, wistfully years later on Pete, credited as chief music writer on no less than six tracks on the album, "He's such a larger than life character, especially on stage. He always was. He's this crazy guy in striped pants running around and lying on the floor. Yeah, you do miss him, but when that lifestyle starts to intrude on the music, then there's a problem. We've always been known as a crazy bunch of guys. We had a reputation in the '70s and that was okay, because the music was still there. However when the craziness starts to outweigh the music, then there's a problem. This has happened with this band at several points, with Michael, with Phil, with Pete, maybe even with me, back in the late '70s at some points when I wasn't playing as good as I could have. People deserve to hear decent music and if Pete's not well enough to perform, then you've got to make a decision. That's what I admire so much about Phil; he doesn't drink at all now. When you've got used to doing something a certain way for so long it's difficult to change that."

As for Way's opinion of the band during this era, he's got mixed feelings, striking a comparison in conversation with Marko Syrjala. "I think the production with Ron Nevison was very important," muses Pete. "Ron and us together at the same time was perfect—he caught the style. I mean he had worked with Led Zeppelin, Bad Company, some very good people and he was able to capture us live but make it sophisticated and fresh. After that, they're very difficult albums to follow up. I would say writing with Paul Chapman was different as well, because it changed the attitude of the writing. It's difficult to put into words, but I would say there are some very good songs on them, but they weren't produced by Ron Nevison. George Martin's a lovely man, but he didn't really capture our rock 'n' roll sound in the same way; it was a lot smaller sound. It wasn't the rock thing that I like and think we get with Ron. Ron could make it sound clean, but also make it powerful. But the Chapman era albums were good and people still ask for those songs."

The record's title track came next, "No Place to Run" being technical and committed heavy metal, a partner in crime to "Lettin' Go" as it were. With its chanted "jungle land" chorus, the song moves like a tank through heavy brush, Phil in his element with a story of an impending, anticipated showdown resulting in violence-splattered mean streets. Of note, Phil at this point was big into Bruce Springsteen, who had to his credit a hit song from 1975's *Born to Run* album called "Jungleland."

Says Phil, "The only thing I remember about the song 'No Place to Run' was George saying, 'Phil, who is this Joey and he's running for the subway?' That was it (laughs). And I said, 'Well, he's like a bloke, innit he? 'E's like a geeza running for the...' (laughs). But I think we had quite a bit of that done before we got there."

Next up was "Take It or Leave It." "I always skip over that track," says Tonka. "Paul had this vision of wanting to be the Rolling Stones, and he would always write those kind of Rolling Stones-type ballads like 'Wild Horses.' It was one of those; Paul didn't really have much and he was feeling a little out so we did that." Phil's lyric charts the sad tale of a rocker off to tour, causing an inevitable disintegration of relations with the gal back home across the sea.

"Now that one I used to like playing live too," says Chapman of "Money, Money." "That song and that album... I think it could have been a little heavier. It's down to production. The album as a whole has a pretty good production; it's unique."

Of crashing closer "Anyday," Tonka offers that, "that's me playing bass, through a Leslie speaker. The only reason I played bass was that, I think, Pete wasn't around the studio at the time and we needed an intro for it. I like Phil's lyrics on that too. His sense of melody I think is great. There's a lot of backwards stuff on that one. And in actual fact, that's another one that didn't get onto the third Lone Star. It never even made it onto the third Lone Star demos, but I have it on tape."

Whatever its origins, the song is a masterpiece, Phil singing a falsetto-marbled break-up blues over stark bass before the band barges in with a bloodied but unbowed series of chords, Chapman then lashing out with a screeching solo before all dies down again. His playing is memorable, melodic, composed... Tonka is the original Slash. Brilliant. Of note, the song fades out right in the midst of expert soloing from Paul, who has said that he recalls being vaguely disappointed with that, adding that, that was one of the two solos he did at Montserrat, the other being "Mystery Train."

Tonka sums up the sonic qualities of *No Place to Run* with the benefit of twenty years of hindsight. "At the time we liked it. Put it like this, nobody went, 'Aw fuck!' although I remember thinking it sounded a little bright. That was another case of the hassles with multiple studios, because we were flying back and forth doing the mixes. That was one of the trickiest ones. When we were touring in Europe and flying back and forth to London, it was snowing in Europe and we were going back virtually every night or every other night to finish the mixing with George Martin in London. And by the time you finish the gig and then you drive to the airport and take off in a two-engine plane in the snow and go across the English Channel from Frankfurt or Luxembourg, and you land at Heathrow and get pushed down the tube and get thrown out underneath the studio... which is exactly where it was. The studio was in Oxford Circus, right underneath the studio is the tube station and you walk upstairs and go into the studio. Under those circumstances, you really haven't got the best ears in the world. So at the time, everyone thought it might have been a bit light at times."

With all these gripes about the sound of *No Place to Run*, my main take-away is an amazement at how differently people hear and frame and describe productions. Personally, I find George Martin's manipulation of *No Place to Run* to be one of the bassiest and most organic of the catalogue, arguably second so far in heft to *No Heavy Petting* which isn't even a Ron Nevison knob-job, but the work of Leo Lyons. If I were to parse the words of these actual band members, I can perhaps find some agreement with them, but only in the guitar department. But if there's any lack of bite or prominence in the guitars, it's only because the bass and drums have been pulled up in the mix. Still, all told it sounds great to me—and strong.

The album would turn out to be the band's most successful on home territory, achieving silver status and a chart placement of No.11, while stalling at No.51 in the US. *No Place to Run* would mark the end of Paul Raymond's tenure in the band (almost to be replaced by John Sloman, ex-Lone Star, ex-Uriah Heep), one that now had lasted through the four biggest records UFO ever had or would have to this day twenty-five years on.

"Actually, to be honest, I saw it as a career move," says Paul. "Because Michael got together with Cozy Powell and I thought, 'This is going to be a really great band; I want to be part of it.' Peter Mensch offered me the gig and it was just too good to pass on. Unfortunately, it didn't live up to expectations. It did very well, but it didn't last. When you try to put bands together, they don't come together naturally. 'Well, we'll have so and so, and we'll have so and so from there... oh yeah, and we'll use Paul too.' I never got on with that bass player, Chris Glen. He was just coming from a different place than me altogether, reading from a different map and I never liked him. It was working under pressure with people that Michael liked."

"He was so talented, wasn't he?" reflects Raymond, on the since deceased Cozy Powell. "Colin Flooks was his real name. He didn't want that to be known, but he's no longer around. Yeah, no-nonsense guy, definitely and a fabulous drummer, possibly the best ever. I never worked with Bonham and I never played with Keith Moon either, but next to those two, he's the man, really."

"I can't honestly say I listened to them," says Paul Raymond dismissively, years later, on the Paul Chapman era of the band in total. "Because I was wrapped up in what I was doing with Michael. But the band did start to go downhill from that point on. I think it got very difficult, because there was a lot of substance abuse and stuff like that going on. But you'd have to ask them about that."

"I heard one of them, *No Place to Run*," once said Mr. Schenker, when asked about the Paul Chapman albums, "and I thought it was going to be great, because George Martin was producing it. But it wasn't. Actually, I didn't hear any of the other albums, even after Paul Chapman left. Even *No Place to Run*, I only heard a few songs. I'm not a consumer, and it's not important for me to know what it is. For me, what's important is to get into the world of creativeness; that's the important part for me. I don't really like to judge either. All I say, when people ask me, I can only express my tastes and my liking, and that doesn't mean anything, really. Basically, as long as people are happy with what they're doing, that's what counts. So if UFO were happy with what they were doing, then that's what counts. The people that liked it, if they were happy, that's what counts. You know, you have a bowlful of fruit, and forcing a strawberry down somebody's throat if you like bananas is a waste of time."

Out on tour the *No Place to Run* tracks that UFO featured live included "Mystery Train," "Lettin' Go," "No Place to Run," "Young Blood," and "This Fire Burns Tonight." What is perhaps the highlight of the record, "Anyday," was not played.

In the meantime, while UFO were touring *No Place To Run* (first before the album was actually out and then in Britain just after Christmas and America through June, Japan in July), Michael was hard at work on his first solo album, a self-titled release as the Michael Schenker Group, or MSG. Curiously, the album could have turned out much different than it did…

"The bass player and the drummer from Rush… they almost worked on my first solo album," explains Schenker. "I visited them at Trident Studios in London, and I don't know what happened. It didn't work out, but they were going to do it, and then something happened. I don't remember what it was. I mean, the whole thing… before I even actually did my first solo album, I was rehearsing with the drummer and the bass player from Aerosmith; they wanted to do it, and we had already rehearsed about four or five songs, and then I think Steven Tyler got well again, and they continued with Aerosmith. And then also Billy Sheehan and Denny Carmassi, the drummer, who was in Heart and Montrose, we also decided to rehearse for three or four months, and that didn't work out. And then finally it was Simon Phillips and Mo Foster of Jeff Beck."

Asked if he actually played with Geddy and Neil, Michael says, "No, we just discussed it and they said they wanted to do it. I think I may have blown it because I made a joke and said that Alex could be the coffee boy (laughs). Maybe I went too far, I don't know. I can't remember actually what happened or why it didn't work out. But it was there, and they wanted to do it and then I don't know what happened."

The producer on board for Aerosmith's *Night in the Ruts* was Gary Lyons, who a couple years later, would be working with UFO on their *Mechanix* record. Recalls Gary, "Joe Perry was in and out, and I was always known as a bit of a prankster. When I was bored, I always try out some practical jokes. And when Perry was out of the band, David Krebs' office wanted Michael Schenker to replace him. And so someone came in the control room and asked if it was okay for Schenker to come into the session. And I said 'Yeah, fine.' And it's always embarrassing when you walk into a recording studio and things are going on. I always feel self-conscious."

"So he walked in, and I just stopped the tape and said, 'Who are you?' 'I'm Michael Schenker.' And he's standing there in black leather, blond hair. And I just told him to fuck off. I called him some Nazi or something and I just told him to get out. And then he left (laughs) and I carried on with the session. And who's the guy who used to work with Krebs who went on to manage AC/DC? The guy with a limp. Anyway, so he came back in, very embarrassed, because I had already told him it was okay for Michael to come in. And he said, 'you insulted' and I said, 'Well, send him back in; I'll apologise.' So he came back in and the second time I said, 'I'm sorry for calling you a Nazi bastard.' And then I said, 'Actually, I'm not sorry. Get the fuck out of here.' So I kicked him out a second time. That's why he never joined the band."

Michael's first solo album, *The Michael Schenker Group*, eventually emerged in August of 1980, featuring hired guns in journeyman Don Airey, bassist Mo Foster and Simon Phillips, a hotshot studio drummer known in hard rock circles for blasting his way through Judas Priest's *Sin After Sin*. On vocals was Gary Barden (from the unknown Fraser Nash), who was the record's only carryover onto the second album.

"Michael couldn't talk English," recalls Gary. "That was actually 1980; his wife at the time was translating all my lyrics into German for him. He needed to understand what I was getting at. But he did understand a couple of my crazy ideas, but not all of them. He actually learned to speak English about a year-and-a half-later, and that was interesting, because he's actually quite a strong personality. I'll give him ten out of ten for doing that. But I think I'm an Englishman, I actually read books and see movies, and I can look at life in the news on CNN and all that sort of nonsense and come up with ideas all the time. For example, 'Lost Horizons' was about *2001: A Space Odyssey*, from 1968. There is this big book I read; I saw the movie. It's about that movie."

That first classic MSG album was produced by none other than Roger Glover. Says Gary, "Roger is a rock god in my eyes. He knows everything about the harmonies; he knows everything about the sounds."

"Working with Gary Barden was great," recalls Michael. "He and I got on very well. I wrote all this stuff ahead of time and then I was looking for a suitable singer. I don't think my manager was too happy with him but I really liked his voice. 'Lost Horizons' was in the first bunch of songs I did for the first solo album, along with 'Into the Arena.' Other than that there's not too much to it."

On the subject of kid-wonder drummer Simon Phillips, Michael comments that, "We rehearsed like three days, and every time we played a particular song, he would play different drum parts. We would do the same songs again, and he would play drums totally different. So basically there was no need for rehearsals because he was always experimenting. It was pretty incredible watching him; very entertaining. Some people don't like his drumming that much, especially for the time. Because he was very free and loose, and in the '80s, drums were very straightforward. But he was very open, adding fills, very unpredictable, definitely exciting, very entertaining to watch."

Chapter Two
The Wild, the Willing
and the Innocent

"Shady characters always popping around the studio"

Following the rich and alchemical *No Place to Run* record with a bit of home-grown, UFO manage to pull a rabbit out of the hat with an album that would be a creative triumph, start to finish, if not much of a commercial barnstormer. Self-produced, *The Wild, the Willing and the Innocent* would become a record as bold as its title, even if the rest of the visuals, namely the album cover, would be a bit of a dud, the typically saucy wrap featuring an obscure shot of a naked woman warmed by a blowtorch. This was barely discernible stateside though, due to the photo having to be muddled to suit milder American corporate tastes.

"It's a basic kind of rock 'n' roll; on the road, 'This Fire Burns Tonight'... sometimes he would pull something out of left field," says Chapman, indicating that this was the record on which Phil bloomed as a wordsmith. "That's why I think *The Wild, the Willing* is my favourite album. Because to me, with things like 'Long Gone,' that's when he started writing in that genre; it's a real street-wise thing. Now, Phil grew up in London in the '60s and I can see why a lot of his stuff is street gang-oriented. That was a big part of his life. In fact, seeing how he is, if he hadn't been in a band, he probably would have become a bit of a villain. I think it kind of saved him (laughs) in a funny way. He draws on that a lot."

As indicated, Paul Raymond, at this point, leaves the band to join Michael in MSG, to be replaced by Neil Carter, ex-Wild Horses. "Neil was a bit like Paul Raymond, a bit like Paul Raymond's understudy," reflects Pete. "Whereas Paul Raymond's got that feel, Neil Carter was a very good musician. To a certain extent, I don't really know how music and songs and characters come into it, but one thing is for sure. The underrated or not in the spotlight-type people like Neil Carter or Paul Raymond... you know, Neil Carter was a very good player and a good guitarist, and an embellishment to the band, so somebody like me could run around the stage and not even play (laughs)."

"Through Phil Collen, Def Leppard," cites Carter, on the dots connecting him to UFO. "I knew Phil when he was in Girl, and I was in Wild Horses and we were both around about the same age, and both around London at the time. I think it was before he was with Def Leppard, but he recommended me to Phil and they got in touch with me and asked me to come down and just sort of play and that was it, really. I don't think they auditioned anyone else apart from me. It was quite nice really, because I had, had enough of Wild Horses by that point. I was looking for something else. It just fell into place really naturally. It was almost decided before I got there that I was going to join them."

"And it was quite funny, because I had to play things like Hammond organ and Moog and that sort of thing and I had never even touched them before (laughs). So I was frantically trying to work out how to work this bloomin' organ thing, before I had my run through with them. I learned a couple of things like 'Only You Can Rock Me' and 'Lights Out,' and I'm quite a quick learner so I just played them through and it was fine. They needed someone who could sing and play guitar as well as keyboards, and I think I was just handy. I was in London and they were in London and it all just sort of worked out fairly well."

Indeed Carter actually fancied himself more so as a guitarist and a singer, telling Dmitry Epstein, "Yes, I was recently looking at a video of the last tour I did with Gary Moore that someone sent me. I remembered I hated that tour as I was chained to the keyboards for most of the night. I liked playing the guitar and having contact with the audience and felt rather frustrated at that time if I remember correctly. I have played lead but long ago and I was okay at it, but my boyhood hero was Mick Ronson who was a great musician, big on sound and flash, but only had a few good licks, really. Having said that, I listen to the Bowie albums occasionally and it still gives me a kick. It seemed the further I progressed, the less lead I did. I did some in Wild Horses and a bit of twin harmony in UFO but to be honest, when you play alongside a guitarist of the calibre of Gary Moore it is neither necessary nor an option."

"They had great delusions of adequacy, those guys," says Carter, tactfully of the notorious Wild Horses. "They were good fun but again, they were terrible wasters, both Jimmy Bain and Brian Robertson. They were characters; let's put it that way. They were great, strong characters, both of them. And again, with hindsight, it's always a learning process. In life, you need people like this. I've worked with some real characters through the years and I can look back on it now and think that they were a bit of a nightmare but it was great fun."

"I did some bits of session work," says Neil, digging back to his musical history before Wild Horses, doubtful that he's on any recordings before that band. "Because of course I worked with Gilbert O'Sullivan, the singer-songwriter, but we never recorded anything. We only did live work. I had a very, very quick intro into it all. I had only left school about a year before and done a load of auditions and had my first professional job within about six to nine months. So I was very lucky. I wasn't one of these people who had struggled for years. I was just in and did it, and got it over and done with by the time I was thirty. It amazes me now (laughs). It was a rapid... not rise to fame, but rise to whatever I was going to do; it was very quick. I didn't have my years of struggling playing in a semi-pro bands."

Making the jump from Wild Horses to UFO was simply a case of opportunity, says Neil. "If there had been an offer I would have gone long before UFO made a move, to be honest. I have to credit them for giving me my first rock break, but Wild Horses were very limited on songwriting ability and were always regarded as a pale Thin Lizzy clone. They were rock 'n' roll with a capital "R" and that led to some crazy times, poor performances and excess as you can imagine. I cannot imagine these days how I got through some of the situations that I was faced with over that period, and in UFO."

As for musical inspirations, keyboard or otherwise, Carter begins with more about his guitar playing. "Yeah, I mean, that's why I'm probably a lousy lead guitarist. Because I listened to people like Marc Bolan and Mick Ronson; these are the people who were my heroes... and Queen, but for different reasons. Queen were my ultimate heroes when I was a kid, and to me... about ticking off boxes in life. When I did the shows with Gary Moore with Queen, in about 1986, '87, their last shows, really, for me, that was it. I didn't have to worry anymore (laughs). That was the apex of my career, the fact that I was sharing a bill, second on the bill to Queen. It was just unbelievable, and to be honest, it was a bit downhill from there."

"But yes, Mick Ronson had a great sound and great rhythm playing. Like I say, he wasn't a particularly great lead guitarist but these were the people I copied and emulated when I was a kid. That's why I've never been a good lead guitarist. I don't know if that was the right pool of people to draw from. I just liked making big crunchy sounds on the guitar. I must say, last week I bought an amplifier, because it's the first time in many, many years where I thought, should I play the guitar? Because the guitar has been in the loft. I've sold all my guitars except two. And I actually bought an amplifier last week. Because the kids have been encouraging me in school (at the time of this interview, 2004, Neil was a music teacher) to do something. So I bought one last week, but I haven't actually plugged it in yet. Never say never."

Neil Carter's stamp wouldn't really be felt on *The Wild, the Willing and the Innocent*, at least compared to his deep writing contribution throughout the subsequent two UFO records. "Actually, vocally, I suppose, harmonies; vocal harmonies," recalls Neil, citing his main inputs into this strident, enjoyable album. "Not much in the way of playing, apart from the saxophone stuff. No guitar at all. Because they had done the keyboard tracks with John Sloman already, so in fact, I did mainly vocal harmonies, many vocal harmonies and the bits of saxophone and that was it, I think. I just sat there while they were mixing it. They had done all the backing tracks by that point, and Phil hadn't done much of the lyrics at that point. So just working really on the final touches of it. I can't remember how much they had done, but I know they had done all the backing tracks."

The John Sloman connection begins with Chapman and Lone Star. However Sloman, then with Uriah Heep, had been recording with the band in the summer of 1980 at Nomis Rehearsal Studios, nearby to where UFO were working. Checking in on what Heep were doing, Phil and Paul eventually had Sloman in for a jam, surreptitiously auditioning him as a possible replacement for Paul Raymond. Offered the job, Sloman turned them down, but not before providing a few keyboard and guitar parts toward the new album. UFO manager Wilf Wright caused a bit of a stink when he released to the press that Sloman was indeed joining the band, after which Bronze Records' Gerry Bron took offence to Sloman even guesting on the record. Things were smoothed over and Bron allowed the cameo, although Sloman's stay with Heep would be short-lived, *Conquest*, issued just after *No Place to Run*, being his one and only with the band.

With regard to actual songwriting, "I began while I was on the road with UFO, really," says Neil, "to give myself something to do on days off. I became aware it was expected of me and I thought I would have a go. Me being me I went at it full steam but it was fulfilling and has been lucrative over the years, too."

"But as I say, they were already most of the way through recording *The Wild, the Willing and the Innocent* when I joined. I think the backing tracks were done and some of the overdubs. They had a bizarre way of working as a lot of the songs were basically written as backing tracks with little or no thought of the melodies or lyrics until Phil actually did the vocals. A lot of the tracks were written and formed in the studio which is rather an expensive way of doing things. Gary was always much more organized and did demos etc. before he set foot in a studio."

"We'd try a lot of things," continues Neil. "My prime instrument when I was in school was the clarinet and one of the things I now teach is the saxophone. It was just trying ideas out. We also had this thing we recorded for *The Wild, the Willing and the Innocent* that had flutes on it and stuff like that, which again, I did. That never saw the light of day. Again, it was just trying different things. When I got into the group, they had a new toy they could play with. So they had this new toy who could play with different instruments and it was just interesting to use things they hadn't used before. So I quite like it. The saxophone didn't sound too bad on it. But Phil was very obsessed, if I remember rightly, by Bruce Springsteen at the time. So I think that's what they were going for with that."

Although the flute was never used, Carter continues to say, "It had some little speaking things in it and Paul did lots of jangly guitar things on it. It's a shame, really. It's quite a sweet little track; I've still got it somewhere. But it really didn't fit. I think because they had the big string things, it was a bit beyond requirement. That was quite an interesting album to record. The finishing touches we did at Air Studios in London. They had worked with George Martin before, and for me it was quite fascinating, because I was sitting there and people like Linda McCartney would be wandering through and listening, and George Martin would come in. UFO was really my first big group, and I was thinking, God, look at these people. I was still very young at that point. Not very young now (laughs). George Martin didn't work on that album, but he was around; he just used to pop in; Air Studios was his studio and he was always there. When we were there, he always seemed to be there."

"Really, effectively, they produced it themselves," adds Neil. "They had a guy there, but they did a lot of it. It was very much done with Paul and myself and Phil and Pete towards the end. They were all taking part in what was going on, and much more so than when they had a producer. The Ron Nevison stuff I think stands out very well because he was a very good producer, and a very good producer in a musical sense as well, in the way that Mutt Lange is, sort of far more along that school of things. Gary Lyons, who did *Mechanix*, wasn't really a producer in that respect."

The Wild, the Willing and the Innocent opens bounding and abounding with "Chains Chains" (keeping the band's round of "doubles" alive), featuring, quite instantly, a dose of huge electric slide, comprising a dramatic intro that gives way to a strong groove and even a stronger riff, offset by a rich, melodic, ennui-laden chorus.

"I always write," noted Pete, when asked about the considerably under-rated track, credited to Way/Mogg. "Certain things I will give to Phil, and Phil will feel the mood and he'll want to do it. It's like, 'I put these chords together because I think you will enjoy them.' It's as simple as that, really. Sometimes he'll say, 'Where are you coming from with that?' I try to write things that are so obvious that somebody can sing to them."

Phil's "Chains Chains" lyric intertwines the tale of Jack the gambler and Jeannie the dancer, both doomed, both victims of betrayed trust. The Bruce Springsteen influence is palpable.

Track two on the record hits even harder, "Long Gone" being one of the band's unsung, under-rated OTT or "over the top" rockers, near speed metal, save for the stealth-like wild west intro, Phil deep into street violence imagery for a second track in a row. One of Phil's best lyrics, the seedy imagery is visceral and motion-filled, as are Phil's portraits of innocence above the fray and hope of escape. Through tender embrace, through casting eyes to the sky, through dreaming, deliverance from this hell just might be in the cards.

The song becomes almost elegant with a half-speed, odd time signature break buttressed by twin axe harmonies, before setting off on a jailbreak once again. "'Long Gone' was a thing I had," notes Chapman. "A lot of these things actually were a hold over from Lone Star, which never got used on *No Place to Run*. The 7/4 chorus in 'Long Gone,' all the guitars (sings it), that was actually all recorded before on a Lone Star track, which I had written; I just brought it with me. It was one of those things I had in a bag on tape, with a lot of the other stuff too."

Pete offers a slightly different tale. "I just remember doing that galloping riff (sings it), in Japan, Tokyo, at the Sun Plaza. As a matter of fact, that's where the song started. I think Paul Chapman got credited for it, actually, but to be truthful, he started playing my riff." Indeed, UFO had played Japan in July of '80, and Pete's tale underscores the assertion by Paul that a lot of the album was written on the road— using Boogie amps and portable tape machines in hotel rooms and such—with the band practically going straight into studio off the exhaustive *No Place to Run* tour.

Strings, a big thing for UFO in the past and indeed within all sorts of rock at the time, through to disco, emerge in surreal and dissonant fashion for the ending of "Long Gone," turning the song into a well-appointed epic. These haunting string arrangements carry gracefully into the intro of the album's title track, a surging hard rocker with a little bit of Phil's Wild West ethic entering the very melodies of the music, even if the lyric charts another murky film noire. The background vocals are courtesy of Neil Carter.

"I recall that the piano part in it was John Sloman, from Lone Star," notes Tonka, correcting, or at least contradicting Neil Carter's memory of things. "Because John was almost in the band at that point. It was in between Paul Raymond and Neil Carter and John came and played with us. I think it was actually John's piano part (sings it), and he was on the demo. But I don't think that's him actually playing. And if I'm not mistaken, if I'm not incorrect, I think it's the brother of Gary Edwards, who started off engineering the album, who actually got fired. He was actually drunk. He had come back from the pub, and I was like, 'How can you even work?' I mean, we have a reputation, but we're the band! You can't have someone behind the desk who's fucked up and falling over."

"So anyway, I believe the piano on *The Wild, the Willing* is Gary's brother, but I can't remember his first name. I remember him in there doing it and we didn't use John now, come to think about it. Phil was actually big into Bruce Springsteen at the time, and he had *The Wild, the Innocent & the E Street Shuffle*, so you can see where that connection came from. And that's how the saxophone got in on 'Lonely Heart' (laughs). Phil was into that whole thing. In actual fact, that wasn't going to be the title track for the album. It was kind of like an also-ran, until it had gotten closer to the end, and then we realised that it was really good and it would maybe give it a little higher profile."

A live rendition of "Long Gone," recorded at the Hammersmith Odeon, January 29, 1981, was added to the 2009 remaster of the album. Also included was a version of "Lonely Heart" from the same show, featuring painfully out of tune vocals and just as dreadful backing vocals. A third bonus track is a serviceable enough "Makin' Moves," recorded at the Marquee, November 15 the previous year.

Unifying the first side of the record like a good Thin Lizzy album is closer "It's Killing Me" (chase with Lynott's "Got to Give It Up"), marking a gradual letdown in heaviness but a sustain in the foreboding, moody, stirring emotion department. As well, Phil is keeping steadfast and resolute to his theme of squalor, the lyric mixing drudgery (through drudge imagery) with the concept of love gone bad.

"'It's Killing Me' was very reflective of the situation at the time we were in," recalls Paul. "I think Phil's words, at that point—and I might even go as far as to say before and after—I think Phil was really shining when it came to coming up with really nifty turns of phrase like 'The thin blue line bends and breaks,' and this kind of stuff. His lyricism was really happening at the time. 'It's Killing Me' was a reflection of what was going on around us. With Paul Raymond going and Neil coming— being honest and not pulling any punches—there was a lot of dope and a lot of drug-related things going on at the time."

"And especially recording most of that in London, because it's kind like the centre of our universe," continues Chapman. "Whereas, if you're in somewhere like Montserrat or Switzerland, you don't really have the seedy side of the city coming out in you. You're working until like five or six in the morning, this kind of stuff. And going in at like half past three in the afternoon and staying in bed all day and shady characters always popping around the studio and this kind of stuff. It was a bit of a London thing, I suppose."

"Another thing I can remember about that song was laying all the harmonies on it, all the guitars. You know, it fades in… it's like a cross-fade from the other song. It doesn't just come straight in like 1-2-3-4; it kind of swells into view. Those were Phil Collen's guitars. Phil was between bands at the time. He had just left Girl before he joined Def Leppard. And I borrowed a Fender Strat off him and I used the Strat to do nearly all the guitars on that. I saw him not too long ago actually. He still has it. And, in actual fact, the amps I used on that were my two main Marshalls. When I endorsed the Vox stuff about eighteen months later, the beginning of 1983, he borrowed my two Marshalls off me, to record, when he was in Def Leppard. And he still has them. When I saw him recently I said, 'Where the fuck are my Marshalls?' And he said 'Oh! I've forgotten about them' and I said, 'Well I didn't!' twenty-two years later (laughs). He says, 'Oh, they're in a warehouse in London.' And I said, 'Well, I'm going over at Christmas, so maybe I can pick them up' (laughs)."

Side two of the original vinyl opens with another strident, expansive heavy metal rocker. "'Makin' Moves' was another Lone Star one— 'Fool's Gold,'" says Paul. "In actual fact, it's identical. The only thing different is the vocals. The actual backing track is almost 100%. It's on the third Lone Star album, the one that Majestic or Shadow had put out (laughs), that I haven't gotten any money for."

Phil's lyric offers an interesting sentiment, Mogg, in the role of narrator, cracking a smile at the way various characters in various tight spots make their moves, how they persevere, how they use what they've got, whether it's wit with the ladies, the guts to commit that crime, or the guts to get up there and rock despite advancing years working against you.

On the subject of songs being left over from the sessions when he was in the band, Paul indicates that there wasn't much but, "there was the odd thing that carried over. Pete used to have this interesting idea which had come up for every album. In the end we used to call it 'The Creeper,' because it would always creep its way in. 'I've got this really good idea.' 'Oh, not that again!' So we'd try to do it again a year later. And the funny thing was, you get an idea like 'The Creeper,' and what ends up happening is that it spawns another idea—'It should go into this.' You end up keeping the new piece which turns into a song and you end up dropping the original idea, which then surfaces on the next album, and then Pete goes, 'I've got this idea.' 'Oh, not that again!' And you give it another try and it turns into something else."

As Paul indicates, "Lonely Heart" features a fair bit of sax, courtesy of new guy Neil Carter. Still, it's a bold, melodic hard rocker, great melodies from Phil, lots of uplift, catchy. It should have been a smash hit; indeed the track was issued as a single, rising to No.41 in the UK charts, backed with "Long Gone." A classic tale of a curious girl who pines for the bright lights and the world of rock 'n' roll, it's actually quite an involved story with lots of lyrics, passages, ambitious arrangements and layering.

"Couldn't Get It Right" is also a melodic hard rocker, with an odd tribal rhythm for the verse, which breaks into another heroic chorus reminiscent of Springsteen, the Stones, but mostly Thin Lizzy. Phil, in a succinct but impressive lyric, laments the soul-destroying wisdom that comes with age.

Closing the album is the record's only ballad, "Profession of Violence," which, at least on the American issue, is called "Profession of," both on the back sleeve and the record centrepiece, to the utter surprise of Tonka, having had that fact told to him in an interview. "It doesn't say 'Violence?' Really?! Good God! I never even knew that. On the British one, I have it up on a frame on the wall at the shop. I'll go have a look at it. Peculiar. Nope. Didn't even know myself."

Nomenclature notwithstanding, Paul recalls the following: "We were in the Caribbean recording *No Place to Run*, and I had written the solo and I'll never forget it. I had an Ovation with a strap on, and I was standing up to my waist in water in the Caribbean, with the fish swimming all around you, beautiful, absolutely gorgeous. Magnificent place. Cried my eyes out when I left there. We were there like seven weeks or something. I had the solo, and I wanted to do something with it on *No Place to Run*. But it was the only time that it had ever worked out that I had written a solo, composed a solo, and didn't have a song for the solo (laughs). So by the time I had actually put the chords to it and turned it into something I could present to the band, we were already doing the next recording. That's how it ended up going on *The Wild, the Willing*. Which of course, we produced ourselves. What we had was a bunch of engineers."

"There was a magnificent note on the end of that song," continues Chapman. "I held the note and where it actually fades, it didn't fade. It was one of those magic studio moments. I leaned over to Steve Churchyard, the guy who was engineering, and I said, 'It would be a shame... it would be something, something, something if that was erased. That would be like a...' And in the middle of the whole thing, he thought that I said, 'We need to erase it' and he said, 'Oh there it is; it's gone.' I said, 'Where did it go?' He said, 'I just wiped it.' 'You did what?! No, I said no! Whatever you do, don't erase it!' I said, 'This is a joke, right? You're fucking around with me here.' He said 'No, it's gone. Honest.' I nearly strangled him! I almost fired him off the session."

"Also, the day that I did that solo was the day I picked up my red B.C. Rich ten-string. I went from the music shop... the guy that ordered it for me, a friend of ours in Tottenham Court Road in London... I caught a cab from there to Air Studios, which is like a mile, straight down Oxford Street, and I took it upstairs, and I took four of the ten off, so it was just a regular six-string guitar. I plugged it in, and that was the first solo that I used that on, was that day, the one that's on the record. That was the very first time I plugged that B.C. Rich in. It became part of my body, like my left arm extension, fantastic. And that's on 'Profession of Violence.' That was based on the book by the Kray twins, London gangsters in the '60s and '70s, and Phil was reading the book at the time, which is called *The Profession of Violence*, and it had quite a deep effect on him really. Because he was walking around talking like Ronnie Kray for a month."

To Phil's credit however, he leaves any concrete information out of the brief lyric, poetically capturing the empty, illusory glory of a violent life but in universal terms.

Back to the album in general, even though *The Wild, the Willing and the Innocent* was quote-unquote "self-produced" it actually sounds quite good, and definitely better than its follow-up, *Mechanix* and arguably the one after that, *Making Contact*.

Plus the songs are superlative. "I really like that one," says Phil, looking back twenty years after the fact. "I enjoyed making that too. We did that up at Air One. That was a fab one because it was during the '80s and we had carte blanche from Chrysalis. That's why we got the string arrangements in and all that stuff. But what we didn't realise was that we were running up a debt. No one pointed that out. 'Oh, what studio do you want? Oh, use our new studio Air London!' which was right slap bang in the middle of Oxford Circus by the tube station, so you could stand up there and survey London from morning to night and there was a pub right around the corner. No one came to see us to say 'How's the album going? What are you doing? Can we hear a few tracks?' They just left us up there and we're like, 'This is fantastic.' We had an engineer and whatever and we were doing this whole thing ourselves. As most people would do, you take your time like you're painting your own house. 'Oh, this is fun, I'm enjoying this.' So we spent weeks up there, and I believe we're still paying for it (laughs)."

Of note, Phil has in fact, semi-consistently in interviews, rated *The Wild, the Willing* as his favourite UFO album, followed by *Lights Out*.

"I think *The Wild, the Willing* was the most expensive," asserts Paul. "The only problem with not having a producer is that nobody is there to kind of crack the whip. When you run over time, you end up changing studios, and when you get to the second studio you go, 'Oh, it sounds much better in here! This guitar sound so much better than the one I had last week. Oh fuck it, let's redo all those.' That's why it came out like it did. You end up running so late though, because nobody is there saying, 'No, that has to do' and there is nobody going, 'We'll fix it in the mix.' And when you're late, you have to leave because there's another band who's had a deposit on the place for nine months or something. I know we went through four studios and it took about two months. I know the main one, which is now part of the Air complex—it was called Wessex at the time—I remember that The Clash had come in and started and finished an album while we were making that, and The Pretenders had managed to come in and do at least half an album as well. And we were still there and went to two or three studios after that."

And Pete? "I thought if it had a bit better production on it, it would've been better. There are some sensational songs on it actually. Ironically enough, on the new Waysted album (*Back From The Dead*, Japanese version, 2004), we're doing 'The Wild, the Willing and the Innocent.' The way I reworked it, I made it more aggressive. I mean, it's quite aggressive anyway but I got rid of all the orchestra and turned it into a hard rock song. It's much more AC/DC than... I don't know, soft rock (laughs)."

"I can remember one time, when Ronnie was in Black Sabbath, they were playing at the McNichols Sports Arena in Denver," says Tonka, recalling a tale from the quite eventful tour for the album, US dates shared with the fledgling Ozzy Osbourne band. "I can remember we went down to the show. I think we were playing there the day after or something like that. We happened to be there; we had a day or two off so we went down to the gig. And whoever was promoting the show, our tour manager, John Knowles at the time, called them up, and they set us up a dressing room with a rider and everything as if we were playing. It was incredible. I'd never met Ronnie before and it was weird, because we were in our dressing room (laughs), when we weren't even playing, because we were going to be there two nights later or something like that."

"And we watched the show—Greg Lake was there; I remember that—and we went down to our dressing room after the gig, Ronnie came in, and it was like as if I'd known him for years. He came up and said, 'Hello Paul, how are you doing?' 'Well, great. Great show.' A real sweetheart, lovely man. I remember that singer, Charlie Huhn. I remember kicking him out of the gig. Somehow or other, he came in and he was fucking trashed and he comes straight into our room and fucking went straight up to this big bottle of Jack Daniels and starts making himself a drink. I'm like, 'Who's that?' Knowlesy went, 'Oh, he's that singer, Charlie Huhn.' I went 'Oh, I remember; he did a review of a single of ours and he slammed the shit out of it,' in Sounds or Kerrang!. So I got him thrown out, being the nasty bastard I was."

"Geezer was a really nice fellow," adds Paul, weaving a typical tale of rock incest. "Geezer used to live in St. Louis. And the singer that ended up in Ghost used to be in Geezer's band, a guy that I grew up with called Carl Sentance. But Carl came to Florida and I found Carl. Geezer left Sabbath or they broke up or something happened; we had the same management company. Geezer was managed by Smallwood Taylor, who also had Maiden, Waysted, Poison, W.A.S.P. and God knows who else. So Carl, the singer for Geezer's band, was living in Cardiff, where I lived in South Wales. We used to go up on the train to London, like all the time. We would plan it so we could travel together. He had a Walkman and he used to give me all the rough mixes of what they were doing in Geezer's band and then I would give him all the rough mixes of what we were doing with Waysted."

"When Waysted went pear-shaped the first time, and I came back to Florida. I was in the same position that I am now, where I had a lot of material and I was looking for a singer. I was going through another divorce, believe it or not. My second divorce. I've had three of them. Four marriages. But I was going through a box of tapes that the old lady had thrown down the end of the driveway for me, and I found this tape that Carl had given me from the train days, and I put it on and it just dawned on me, 'Ha! Carl, that's the singer I need.' So I got somebody in England to get hold of him, and he called me up and I said, 'Do you want to come to Florida and do some recording?' And he said 'Yep, I'll be there tomorrow.' And that was it. I went to pick him up and he became part of the thing. But he used to come down to the shows with Geezer whenever we would play St. Louis. Geezer knew Pete and Phil, and I knew Carl. But no, super guy, real nice fella."

Two months after the Sabbath liaison in May of '81, UFO was off to Spain, for some bullshit sessions with Rainbow. Tonka explains: "With Rainbow, we did a couple shows in America, but we also co-headlined some bull rings in Spain. We did it over the course of two weekends. Def Leppard opened, with Pete Willis and when Rick still had two arms. Phil Collen wasn't in the band yet. One night we headlined and the next night they headlined; this was Rainbow with Joe Lynn Turner."

"The first fucking gig... we got there, and these bullrings are smelly, horrible places, right? Phil had his girlfriend with him, a Texas lady,

Jean; I think she's dead now. And where all the tents were, because there aren't really any dressing rooms at bullrings, it stinks like shit everywhere, and they put these tents up for guitar tuning rooms, and they've got tents for the food. The promoter puts on the local food for the band and crews, and Phil was standing behind Jean queuing up to get something to eat at this big long table. She was hammered and the Spanish lady said something to her. Jean actually came back with a bit of a mouthful, and then the woman started shouting at Phil, because his girlfriend is a pig."

"Then the next thing you know, there was this guy called Ian (Broad), who was Ritchie Blackmore's tour manager, standing behind him, this guy from Liverpool. All of a sudden this huge fucking fight erupts and Phil is punching the fuck out of this Ian guy. Joe Elliott and I are standing there going, 'Well, look at this.' Food going everywhere. This is before the first gig, the very first day of the eight shows. It's like, okay, better move these guitars. Joe is handing off guitars. I had just tuned every single one of them, with my guitar techs. And they fucking went flying into my tuning tent and smashed everything everywhere. I mean, you're talking blood and teeth. They were really going at it. So the next thing you know, it gets broken up. And Phil ends up doing the gig with two black eyes and the other guy had a broken shoulder or something like that. The very first gig. Ritchie is nowhere to be found. He's run away and hidden."

"But we all have to stay in the same hotel that night," continues Paul. "So when we get to the hotel, obviously they tried to keep everything as separate as possible, like 'quick, get him upstairs in case he sees him in the bar.' I don't know how it happened, but Phil had this .357 with him, on the road in Europe, which was absolutely stupid. And I remember he had one in America. There's actual pictures of him up on the UFO website, with Phil and his gun and his cowboy hat, with Jean, that lady, thinking he was John Wayne or something."

"It wasn't loaded and we were in my hotel room. I had this massive boombox, this huge friggin' blaster. It's after the gig, there's a bottle of booze there or something, and something is on extremely loud, something that Pete was probably playing; I don't know. And there's a bang bang bang bang bang on the door. And, hey, check this out, Phil had got his gun. I said, 'I'll do the door open; you go "Freeze!"' So we did (laughs). So there's the bang bang bang bang on the door, I'm standing behind the door and I pull it open quick and Phil goes 'Freeze!' Ritchie is standing there. With this gun pointed straight at his head. He had monogrammed pyjamas on—RB—and they're like pale blue or something. He went like, 'Ha.' His face just went ashen, white, like the colour my refrigerator, and his jaw dropped, and Phil went, 'Oh, sorry' and Ritchie went, 'Uh, er, ah...' He didn't know what to say. 'I thought it was my crew being really loud and obnoxious.' 'Well it's not, is it? Shut the door.' I was like, wow! You don't see that everyday, you know? (laughs)."

"Anyway, the next day, of course, all the hotels had to be changed, because they wouldn't have us staying in the same hotel. But Joe Lynn Turner came over to the hotel, the second or third night, because he wasn't really involved in anything that had happened and he was over trying to find some stuff. So we kept sending him up to the 14th floor of the hotel, and room 1427. There're nine floors in the hotel. Stuff like this. I mean, we were awful to him; we really were. I can remember we were doing one of the other gigs and he was outside with some Spanish woman, and he couldn't get in to the gig and he never had a pass. We were standing behind the door in this bullring arena, and you could hear, 'Hey man, my name's Joey. I'm the singer in the band. Let me in!' This was going on for ages, and we didn't say anything to anybody. 'Hey, check this out; he can't get in to the gig.' And they were getting ready to go on, and they're like, 'Where the fuck's Joe?' And he's outside going, 'I can't get in!' Security were really assholes. But there were a lot of memorable things on that set of gigs."

Fortunately things smooth themselves out after awhile. "Yeah, I believe they did," laughs Paul. "As I say, it was only about nine days. But then we played with them in America. I remember doing Alpine Valley with them, which is a big show just north of Chicago. It was the place where Stevie Ray died in the helicopter, East Troy, Wisconsin, a big open-air like Pine Knobs, Irvine Meadows. It's like 6,000 seats with the grass and it's a natural amphitheatre. We did two nights there with them. I think Molly Hatchet might have opened, and then it was us and Rainbow. I did actually speak with Ritchie and said sorry about the pyjama thing. He showed me his rig. He showed me how he used a tape echo, in between our sets. He was a pretty nice guy. He seemed on the level. I hear a lot of stories about him being arrogant, a bit of a bastard sometimes or whatever. But no, he didn't seem like that all. Maybe the gun thing mellowed him out."

"Oh God, did he tell you about the fight?!" exclaims Neil Carter, when the infamous bullring story is brought up. "And did he tell you about me trying to tune the guitars, holding the dressing room up? Because

Phil—it's usually Phil—was fighting some character. I'm standing there with these guitars and the dressing room was suddenly collapsing in on me. That was a bizarre experience, but again, it's all alcohol-fuelled. I think Phil always had this thing about Ritchie Blackmore; I don't think he was very keen on him. But there were not that many people that were keen on Ritchie Blackmore. But I think there was always this underlying feud or feeling of unease and I think it just boiled over. I think it was the tour manager he was having a ruckus with. So yes, that was quite unpleasant."

"And also going out on stage and realising that the power was half power and that the Hammond organ was in a completely different key to the rest of the band. So you were standing on stage starting with 'Only You Can Rock Me' and suddenly I was playing in a completely different key to the rest of the band. It had something to do with the power being stranger and for some reason the organ was in a different key. I never understood why, but we were just in a different key. Phil and Pete seemed to be a bit mean to Joe Lynn Turner, if I remember rightly. I don't think I've even actually said two words to Ritchie. Ritchie was one of those people who tended to just come in and out. But the other guys in Rainbow, like Don Airey and Roger Glover, they're all people we knew from being on tour and doing festivals."

"Lots of heroin," recalls Tonka, when asked how bad things had gotten with drugs during his tenure in the band. "Yeah. Lots of heroin from the year... whenever we headlined the Reading Festival, Neil's first show, 1980 (note: immediately subsequent UK touring was supported by Fist). From 1980 until the end. Nothing before that, really. But it was peculiar how it worked out, because everybody around us was doing it. It was one of those things. No matter where you went, it was always there. When you went to Europe or touring, then obviously, it has to stop. Because you can't just turn around and buy heroin in Poland. But whenever we'd get back to London, it would be pretty full-on."

"After awhile, you start functioning on it. It just becomes the normal thing, and that's when it's really hard to stop. When you end up going on the road, or you're going to Greece or America or Canada or Japan, then you really have a problem. It takes two or three days for it to... you know, everybody in the band is really ragged because they're all coming off. Andy never did. Andy smoked his way through pounds and pounds of weed and drank wine, and he was probably the most level-headed person in the band. Which is why he gets the brunt of all the jokes. Phil will do it to death. Yeah, I've been in pubs with Phil when he's nodded out completely into a coma. He sat there with his hand on a pint of beer and he'd just nodded out and you can't wake him up. And it would be embarrassing sometimes because there are people around that you didn't want seeing us like that."

As for whether the band's abuse of substances ever affected the band live, Paul figures, "Not really, maybe once or twice. Phil would have to have a sit on the drum riser, like at Hammersmith one time, which was a bit embarrassing. No. I can remember playing on my birthday once, at the Agora in Columbus, for the King Biscuit Flower Hour. And we went on at 11:00 in the morning or something stupid like that, because it was a day show to be simulcast or whatever. And I can remember we were drinking beforehand and it was like, wow, this better slow down really quickly, because this is in the one you can't fuck up. Because this is going out on the radio everywhere (laughs). And I've since listened to the broadcast and I can pick things out, but I don't know if anybody else could. You'd have to really know the band and to be at a wad of shows every night."

"There were a few instances of people falling over, like Pete running to the front of the stage and not knowing where the end was and going straight down the pit and pulling all his gear over because he was still plugged in. Broke his leg in Columbus. Columbus again—which is where he lived for awhile—in Waysted, where he jumped off the stage a little bit too over-enthusiastic about something and fell down between two flight cases and broke his leg—and kept playing the gig!"

"And I jumped off the drum riser once and busted all my ankles up. But that didn't have anything to do with being out of it or whatever. We could have tightened up a few things. But we used to tour and play so much that it was like a second nature thing in the end. Between Pete and I, it was like unspoken choreography. It was something where we could read each other. As soon as you walk up the back of the steps of an arena while the intro tape is on, it's like you click into a different mode of thinking. We would all huddle and we would psych ourselves up like we were the Dallas Cowboys or something and bash each other on the palms, one up, boom! And then you emerge out of it an hour and 45 minutes later and it's back to that again."

"We used to fight from time to time," replies Paul, on the subject of Phil and violence. "The first gig in Poland we had a fight. Yeah, the very first gig. Billy Sheehan was standing there going, 'What the fuck have I got myself involved with?!' And Phil was hitting Jean, his girlfriend, because she had taken all the methadone while we were onstage.

Something like that. Some nonsense going on. And he had her over a table. So I jumped on him, and the next thing you know we're rolling in all the Polish rider, like sardines on toast. Yes, the Polish rider. Yeah, we had a few. But Phil was the nicest bloke in the world. If he didn't have a buzz or he wasn't pissed-off, he was super. And after, he'd always cry, 'I didn't want to do that!' Oh Christ, here we go again."

"Even in the early days, in 1973, when we used to play pubs around England, I can remember him getting into fights. A roadie he'd beaten up actually sued him once. I think it was Nottingham Boat Club, where we were banned, because Phil had hit the manager or the owner. Something to do with money; I don't know what it was. I mean we're talking thirty-something years ago. There was a pretty heavy one in France as well. He actually jumped off the stage and went up and nutted a promoter right in the mouth and broke his two front teeth and then jumped back on the stage and continued the song. And then after we left the gig, two guys who were working for the promoter went and hit two of our road crew with a chain, while they were getting in the truck. They had to have stitches down the back of their heads. Yeah, stupid. It was absolute nonsense. I don't even know why... somewhere in France."

And how about drama between yourselves? "Not so much on stage, but there were some heavy moments. Phil and I had a few fights. But we're best of friends now. I was over at Phil's house in October. Usually, we can't remember what we were arguing about, and that's usually how the arguments occur. And then the next day everybody is crying on everybody's shoulders. There was usually large amounts of intoxicants involved. It's very rare that it was musical."

Paul then goes on to give a sense of the evolution of the band's live show, through his joining for *Strangers of the Night* through to the end of his tenure.

"When I helped the band in 1977, when Michael went AWOL, it was primarily like a club thing, and maybe some theatres, playing with people like Johnny Winter, and really bizarre billings. But we did do Soldier Field, which is like one of the last gigs. And then we all went back to London. I was going back to Lone Star, to tour for the second album. So I had to split. And then when I went back in '78, Phil picked me up. They had moved to Los Angeles and it was still kind of a club thing. But we actually went out supporting Rush, and it elevated into an arena thing. I remember that very first gig in Market Square Arena, I think in Indianapolis, and it was like, 'Fucking 'ell, this is cool as hell.' We did like 50 shows with them or something, right up to Christmas, from Halloween to Christmas and then I went back. My wife was in Holland, and we had a place in London. We moved back in January to Los Angeles, because the band was now based in L.A. and then I got a place to live."

"Then it started getting to the point where summer was coming and we were doing more open air shows, bigger shows, and that opened the door bit, especially with the George Martin album, *No Place to Run*, when we came back after the album, the first official tour of the new band. As opposed to *Strangers*, where we weren't actually going out and playing new stuff. *Strangers in the Night* had just been released and we were doing most of the material from that. So there wasn't any new material of mine in the thing. Then it got the point where we were doing arenas ourselves. And for the next couple of years, I would say it wasn't themed, but the rigs seemed to grow, every tour. I mean, at one point, we had five semis or something like that, which, for back then was just fucking staggering. For a PA system, we would always have the best and biggest Tasco sound system, and the lighting thing, I mean, it was really, really growing. But it really wasn't themed. Looking back, it could've been."

One of the biggest shows the band ever played was Day on the Green in Oakland, California, with REO Speedwagon and Kansas, to a crowd of 70,000. At this show however, Tonka was having technical difficulties and smashed his guitar to bits at the end of the set. The very largest however was in L.A, at the World Music Festival, to a crowd estimated at 125,000. Bill mates included 38 Special, Toto, Van Halen and Aerosmith.

"There was an Aztec backdrop, plus a big plain UFO one," continues Paul, further charting the course of the band's visuals. "There was a black one. But we had five... they were kind of termed gantries. They were huge trusses but not just trusses that would go up and across the stage but they were up behind it. And Martin Nicholas, our lighting guy, who ended up going to work for Maiden... I'm actually still in contact with him now; I speak to Martin all the time. He could spell out letters in the lighting colours (laughs). And his favourite one was 'Martin Nicholas,' this kind of stuff. You wouldn't really notice it unless you would go... and I'd be back standing at the sound desk, and Martin would be up testing his lights for the day and I'd go, 'You fucking jam! Look at the...' and it would be subliminal: 'Martin Nicholas.'"

"But there were a lot of things that would happen. Like, we were one of the first bands to use Vari-lites. At one point, we had four guys up in the rig with Super Troupers, which even then... I mean, I went to see Metallica recently, and they have only four now. It was quite a spectacle. Super Troupers are the things that normally go at the back of an arena, the big follow spots that look like cannons and you could put different colours in them. We actually had them up in the rig. I mean, it's really very impressive. But we never used to use pyro. We tried it once and it was a total disaster. I remember the first gig I did with them back in England on the *Strangers in the Night* tour, we decided to use dry ice. Let's try some dry ice, or some fog and dry ice, something like that. And the band couldn't see each other for like ten minutes. Unbelievable. And we finished the thing, and Phil says, 'Now you know why we never use effects like smoke or dry ice.' It was bad news, hilarious."

While UFO were going about their business, Michael Schenker offered up (in September of '81) his second MSG album, this time with UFO acolyte Paul Raymond as part of the mix, along with Gary Barden from the first MSG, new bassist Chris Glenn and new drummer Cozy Powell.

"You're talking actually British and British here," says Barden, comparing Powell to the first record's Simon Phillips. "Cozy, in my books, was actually a great live impresario; he did the '1812 Overture' with the lights and explosions. He knew that. It was incredible; the kids absolutely loved it. Simon, he was like 20 at the time, I think. He was into the technicalities at the time—he's a lot more of a jazz-oriented drummer. I mean, he's a genius as well; both of them are actually geniuses. I can't actually put the two side by side; I can't do that. And Chris Glenn... I mean, I loved the Alex Harvey Band. Chris and Ted McKenna did a couple of years with MSG. Chris, he's a very complicated character. I'm not saying in which area he's actually complicated in (laughs). Because I can't—I need a lawyer! But obviously, Chris is a great bass player, solid as a rock, and it was a pleasure to actually play with Chris."

Says Michael, rightly, on the cloggy, loggy, soggy sonic quality of the second MSG record, "You know, when it happened, I wasn't happy with it, because I knew that Ron Nevison could do better than that. Cozy Powell wasn't happy; he had to remix it. We wanted more room and he mixed it by himself and when he presented it to us, you know... Cozy was very unhappy with it and we had to remix it. I think the songs are excellent, but production-wise it could have been better."

Chapter Three
Mechanix

*"There's a pub in Switzerland
better than the one we use in London"*

In February '82, UFO returned with *Mechanix*—a bit of a dog's breakfast as they say, yet an album that really has no problem winning a UFO fan over given a little effort on the part of the (open-minded) listener. The songs are good, if, on balance, a little poppier than the sum total of its cohesive, edgy, full-bodied predecessor. In fact, both the rockers and the ballads, not to mention all those happy and accessible hard rockers in between, seduce with varying degrees of charm.

Pete Way has always been kind of hard on the record for its poppiness, so much so, that he would be dashing off to form Waysted when it came time to do *Making Contact*. Remarks Pete, "Around about that time, it was a bit like... I wouldn't say a job. But it was like, 'Oh great, we're going to go to Switzerland to record. Oh we're going to go there.' We try to make everything pleasant, enjoyable. So it's like, oh that's good, there's a good pub up there. Oh, that pub's better. There's a pub in Switzerland better than the one we use in London. I like the London one as well. *Wild, Willing* was London and *Mechanix* was Switzerland. You get your environment and your atmospheric going for yourself. I like *The Wild, the Willing* because it was more raw. Having said that, it could've been a lot better with a really good producer like Mutt Lange, who we never managed to work with."

The brunt of the album was indeed recorded at Mountain Studios in Switzerland, but additional recording was also done at The Manor in Oxfordshire, plus Scorpio Sound and Maison Rouge in London, with the mastering handled at Sterling Sound in New York.

"At the time it would've been great, had we done that. *Mechanix*... Gary Lyons had done Foreigner. Which was good, but he didn't really put that much into it. What I didn't like about that sort of thing was that it was like, let's try and write a single. And I hate that 'let's try and write a single syndrome'. There were bands like say Styx, and I hate using the name because I don't like to call characters out, but I look at them and I go, I detest everything about this, and you look at them and I would say that if the record company is asking you to be like something you detest, then you tend to do it with less enthusiasm. So in my circumstances, I liked being on tour and I thought that's what the band were all about. And if I had to be like Styx, that's not what I'm about. But on that album, you know what? Nothing wrong with the songs. It's just the attitude of looking for a hit single. Because it's hard to imagine Malcolm and Angus Young sitting around trying to write the next hit single, you know what I mean? That I admire. I admire the integrity and I admire the style and I don't like copying."

Continues Pete, "Once you switch from Michael to Paul... some people say they prefer some of the albums that Paul Chapman played on. If we ever missed the mark, it was because somebody said, 'you have to come up with more hit singles.' I mean, we really didn't ever try to bend ourselves that way but sometimes you get a situation where you're forced to get a little more that way. It was like a disappointment to the record company if you didn't come up with something that maybe Foreigner might have come up with. That's not bad in essence, but it can affect you."

The irony of Pete calling *The Wild, the Willing* "more raw," is that *Mechanix*, by virtue of the record's muddy, almost botched production, is actually rawer than the self-produced predecessor by most definitions of the term. One senses that Pete's disdain is directed more toward this idea of "hit single syndrome," as well as a few other fey moves, like the saxophone, as Paul Chapman will confirm.

"What happened on *Mechanix*," begins Paul, "there are two things here. One of them is partly my fault and one of them is partly Neil Carter's fault. Where my fault comes in—and it has nothing to do with the music—if you look at the Lone Star albums, the first one is produced by Roy Thomas Baker and it was engineered by Gary Lyons. The second album was produced and engineered by Gary Lyons. I really liked the way Gary Lyons worked. Gary Lyons produced *Mechanix*. When the list of producers came up for *Mechanix*, we said, 'Listen to Gary's stuff,' and they all said, 'Yes we like that; this is really good.' And

I said I would put my neck on the line. I know Gary and he's very creative and he's not so much aggressive. He's a great guy to get along with, and he's a fucking nutcase, but in a funny way. So I was all for it, plus I wanted to see him again (laughs). He's a really nice guy. So anyway, Gary became part of the thing."

"As well, it was Neil Carter's first full-blown album, because with *The Wild, the Willing and the Innocent*, he was in right at the end. So Neil's involvement at this point was a little heavier. I had moved to Florida at this point and I was going through a divorce with my first wife, and my writing… my quota wasn't met, due to various reasons. Normally I had more than enough, but Neil had a lot more, so a lot of it went in Neil's direction, hence Neil played saxophone. And Phil was into Bruce Springsteen at the time and he said, 'Sure, saxophone, let's use that.' And next thing you know, Neil's stamp is a little more on it. It kind of pissed Pete off, so much so that in actual fact he left. But it was softer songs and this and that. In actual fact, on my anthology, there's nothing on there from *Mechanix*. And that was because of choice because of all the songs I liked, I couldn't find any on there that were up to the power of the ones before or after."

"The funny thing is, getting back to Gary's involvement, we were writing down at a place near Bath, in Hastings in the south of England. One day, if I remember right—we did the thing in Switzerland—before we left, I was down there one night with Andy, and we were playing through the PA, *Firing on All Six*, and Gary came down with his wife, who he wasn't married to when he did the Lone Star stuff. I had never met her before and he looked at his wife and said, 'Wow, I haven't heard this for years!' And he said right there in front of everybody, 'Now that was in the day when I used to be a producer!' And I looked at Andy and I went, 'What?! What does that mean? Is he trying to tell us something?'"

"Gary actually doesn't do anything in the music business anymore. It was the start of Gary's decline from abuse. Gary was one of those classic situations of too much too soon. He went from the tape-op engineer to all of a sudden producing Foreigner's first album—'Feels Like the First Time,' 'Cold as Ice'—to working with the Rolling Stones, all that stuff, working with a lot of these different people. And he became so complacent. We couldn't get Gary to work in the end. We had a great time with him. So when all was said and done, we were late, which we usually used to be. We would be on the road when we were mixing. We'd be in Europe and we'd be flying back and forth and that gets hairy. You finish playing in France and have to go back to London in four hours and then you have to be back in Milan to play and this went on for weeks. So you would get burned out pretty quickly."

"I had worked with Paul in Lone Star," begins Lyons, at the time of my interview with him, 2007, deep into the catering business in Manhattan (of note, Gary is of no relation to Leo Lyons, producer for UFO in the '70s). "When Paul went to UFO, I worked with him in that band. Great guitarist. UFO I took to Switzerland to work out of Queen's studio. The UFO guys, like the Foreigner guys, they have experience and they tend to let producers do what they need to do. The young artists always accuse producers of fucking with their art. You ask them to do something, and it's always 'Why?' as opposed to just doing it."

"When I was asked to do UFO, they had their manager... we called him Seldom Right—Wilf Wright, and without going into too many details, it seemed like a good idea to get the guys away from bad influences. So I suggested taking them to Switzerland, so they would be better behaved. So I called up, I forgot who, one of the guys in Queen. I think it was Roger Taylor. And I said that I wanted to book the studio in Montreux, to take the band there. And he said, 'Well, you know, you have to talk to...' their manager at the time? I don't remember. It was after they'd finished with John Reid. And he (Jim Beach) was like their accountant or something, who took over as their manager."

"So I was trying to work out what the budget was. It was Chrysalis back then, and they were on a very tight budget. But by the time I had called whoever the Queen manager was, they said, 'What is your budget?' And I said, 'Well, I can afford to pay...' and I don't remember the number, but hypothetically, ten or £20,000, for the studio. And they said fine. And I said, 'That's it—fine?' And he said, 'Yes, the band told me that whatever price you wanted to pay is fine. Whether it was nothing, and upwards. You can have the studio for anything.' Because I had helped them in the day when they were stuck in their Trident deal. So that was pretty cool. So UFO reaped the benefit of that."

And then it came time to corralling the herd of chickens that was UFO in the notorious Tonka era.

"They were crazy, but that was the business back then. You just had to work around certain situations and get the best out of people at the right time. That's about it. There was a lot of picking on the drummer. He was an easy target for practical jokes. And that album, if I remember correctly, that was one of the best ones for practical jokes going on all the time. I tied some kippers to the manifold. Have you heard that one?

When he went over to the car, the garage? And they were laughing at him. And he's going, 'I don't think that's funny!' Okay. And I was doing lots of tricks with him in Montreux. I don't know if I want to go into them (laughs). But there's a lot of practical jokes."

"The kipper story," laughs Andy. "I remember, this was when I came up to do some overdubs. I drove up to the studio from London; I'm staying with my parents near London. So I went back to Oxford, rented a brand new Volvo. I think they were doing some mixes up at The Manor, and I drove out there for the day—Mick Bolton, the original guitar player, came with me. I was hanging out with him; he's my mate. I had to do some tom-tom overdubs or something. But knowing Gary, it might've been a whole ruse just to get me up there."

"But I did these overdubs, and he said, 'Go off and have some fun.' They had this go-kart track at The Manor. So we went out on these go-karts and we're playing around, me, Mick, and a friend, and I said, 'Do you need me?' 'No, I think it's sounding good; go and have some dinner and then you can go.' So we stayed for dinner, and then we got in our car, and we were partying pretty hard back then. We started driving home, and it smelled like really dead fish in the car. So I'm thinking, bloody hell, they must've been cooking fish in the kitchen, because the car was parked at the back of the kitchen. I'm thinking, the guys aren't going to like this, because this is a brand new car."

"The further we drove, the worse it got! And we thought, this is ridiculous, it stinks in here! Something just clicked deep in the back of my mind. I remember Gary telling me this story about when he took a few frozen kippers and wired it onto someone's exhaust pipe, and how as the car got hotter, the kipper would start to cook. I went over and looked, and as luck would have it, a filling station's coming up. It's about 1:30 in the morning, and we had been partying. I shouldn't have been driving, but in those days you kind of did."

"We pull into this station and I had to fill up, and thinking I've been stitched-up, I know what this is. And there's one little guy in the kiosk where the gas pumps are, and standing next to him was the typical British Bobby with his bicycle. So I guess he's on his rounds and he used to stop and check on the guy in the filling station. So I'm thinking, oh fuck, this is going to the good, policeman at the station. And as we slow down, you can see all the smoke billowing out the side of the car."

"I pulled out a bit from where they were and got out of the car. The two other guys, Mick and John, were actually creasing up laughing, because at this point, I'm saying, 'Gary fucking stitched me up.' So I raise the bonnet of the car, and there's all this smoke out there. This car had loads of room in there, and I can see this plastic bag full of kipper fillets that was expertly wired to my exhaust manifold. I'm looking over to the guy, you know, can you help me? 'Have you got a problem?' 'No, I'd just like to borrow a pair of pliers or wire cutters.' 'Why, what's wrong?' 'Well, I've got a kipper wired to my exhaust pipe.'"

"And he looked at me, and in a minute, the copper's going to say, 'Would you like to blow into this?' But they just looked at me, and I kind of scooted under the car with some wire cutters. But man, that car stank, and I had to take it back. I just had to drive it in there with the windows open, and said to the guy, 'It's full of petrol; here's the mileage,' and just got out of there as fast as I could. I don't think that car would've ever been the same again. That was Gary. Gary was always good for a laugh."

"On *Mechanix*, I did a lot of the actual orchestral scoring," continues Gary, somehow back to business. "So I did the arrangements, when we brought in orchestras on these things. Plus I did co-write a couple of the songs with the band. There's a fine line between the producer's input and when you actually start writing whole passages. But I used to get involved in working on the lyrics or the melodies or the structures of songs."

Asked if there's a Gary Lyons sound, or a deliberate producer's philosophy, Lyons says, "I don't know; I can't answer that. I just recorded it as I heard it. I tended to go into each album with how I want the thing to end up. But you always start with a blank canvas. I could come up with a bunch more clichés but that's pretty much it (laughs). You go in and you work with what you've got. Each band has their own sound and style and you just try to enhance it."

On the subject of whether he played an instrument himself, Gary figures, "Well, back then I played a lot of things. I haven't picked anything up in quite awhile. But keyboards, guitar, bass. Not proficient, but enough to sit down and show somebody what to play. Or to write sections of songs and play them."

"We always ended up running overtime and over budget," continues Paul Chapman, underscoring the perennial UFO theme of excess over success. "It's a standard thing; it's what bands do. Nobody ever brings the album in under budget. Or nobody ever brings the album in with time left to go. 'Oh, there's four days left in the studio. Oh, let's do something else.' You know what I mean? It never works like that. And when we were doing that, there was really nobody around to crack the whip. So you'd run overtime in the studio and somebody would go, 'Oh, Duran Duran are booked in the studio tomorrow. So we have to go somewhere else.' And then you'd have to set everything up in the new studio and this happened four times in the whole thing. So when it came to mixing, we were almost ready to go on the road and the album wasn't even out. So it was late doing it. I wouldn't say it was a rush mix, but I think more of it was left to Gary. We weren't around as much as maybe we could have been."

"With *Mechanix*, I think we should have carried along the same line we did with *The Wild, the Willing*, and the reason I think *The Wild, the Willing* came out like it did, we had no producer. It sounded really good. The first thing you do when you finish the drum tracks is you lose the drummer—last thing you need. Nothing against Andy, but drummers in general—Dixie Lee in Lone Star, Jerry Shirley when we did *The Good, the Bad, the Waysted*—the first thing you do is send them home. Because they don't think notes, they don't think musically, they think percussion and they think hits. The only thing they are concerned with is if you can't hear the snare drum, then they come in and turn it up and they're always playing around with drum sounds and it's like, 'Look, get the fuck out of here.'"

"So then it's left to whoever is left in the band," explains Paul. "Okay, when we would mix, especially *The Wild, the Willing*, the mix is basically down to me, Phil and Pete, because there was no Paul Raymond, you know what I mean? Now if you listen to our last Waysted album, *Save Your Prayers*, the mix was down to me and Pete and Simon Hanhart, so I think a large portion of *The Wild, the Willing*, when you write the song you can actually hear the song in your head. You hear the chords and you say this key would fit and this melody would fit here and I can change the tempo here. You pretty much envisage the whole thing in your head."

"So the hardest part of songwriting is to get it out of your head and onto the album. And how the hell do you do that? Well, the first thing you need is other players and you need to communicate with those other players. This is how I think this should go and they subtract and add. Pete and I always have this thing where I would say, 'I can hear that,' and he would say, 'Yeah, I can hear that too.' And when you get in the studio you have to situate the things—where do I put his mic etc.—and eventually you mix the whole thing together. If you know how to do that, the musicians will always produce better stuff than the producer, unless the producer is as good as those guys, from a musical and visionary point of view. I think that is where Gary let *Mechanix* down."

"I quite like *Mechanix*," volunteers Neil Carter, confirming Paul's assessment of his deep contribution, "only, really, because it was the first time where I had been seriously involved in writing songs and been involved with the whole production of it. We recorded it in Montreux, Queen's studio and I'd always been a great fan of Queen. It was actually very fulfilling just to be in that space. It was the first time where I had actually actively written songs and been involved with it. Because up to that point, when I joined UFO, they had already been recording *The Wild, the Willing and the Innocent*. So then I just threw myself into it wholeheartedly, because I had all these ideas, because I had never done any of it before. So I was just beavering away while we were on tour. I used to have my guitar and my little mini studio, and I would write. Certain things have seen the light of day that I didn't use with UFO, when I was with Gary Moore. One song in particular, 'Empty Rooms,' which I recorded with Gary Moore, turned out to be the most lucrative thing I've ever done in my life and it bought my house, you know what I mean? (laughs); it did great things. So UFO was like the beginning of it."

"Just being brutally frank," continues Neil, "UFO were the biggest wasters of money on the planet; we never really went into the studio with much in the way of ideas. We were actually writing while we were in Montreux, costing goodness knows what a day. So no wonder UFO never actually made any real money—they used to waste so much of it. It was only when I went with Gary Moore that I realised that they were so switched on to these things and they never wasted a penny. And that's why Gary was in the position he was financially. Whereas UFO had always been just wasters. So we went in to record *Mechanix* with very little material actually formulated into songs. Phil would come up with the lyrics at the eleventh hour. I wrote quite a lot of the vocal melodies on *Mechanix*; Phil would just put the words to the stuff that I came up with. Not all of it, but the stuff that was my melodies. But I don't think it's a particularly well-produced album, to be honest. I think *Making Contact* is a much, much better produced album. Gary Lyons' production wasn't good. It was okay, but it probably wasn't worth the money that they had paid him to do it. In retrospect, it's not a great sounding album."

Dealing with the slight contradiction there, one might surmise that Neil indeed came with songs, but that being the new guy and only one part of a five-man team, that still meant the band was their typically unprepared selves. Graphically proving the point, Carter is in on fully six of ten of the *Mechanix* writing credits.

Paul Chapman essentially says as much, continuing to set the stage for this oddly soul-searching record. "The main thing I remember about *Mechanix* is that I really didn't have much of an input in the thing as I did the other records. Because Neil had come in and that was one of the reasons that Pete ended up leaving the band. Because it ended up going... I'm not going to say that it turned into the Neil Carter show, because it really didn't. But the influence was there and he was subtly pushy, which I think was another thing that eventually pissed Pete off. All the ideas were Neil's."

"I think if you look at the Waysted records, that's more where Pete and I were wanting the band to be at. At the time, I'd just moved back to Florida and I was going through a bad divorce here, with my first wife who is Dutch. It was very tricky. The time that I would normally put to one side to write... I had a set-up, back then. You had like a Revox and I'd take my Boogie amp home, and that was about all. It wasn't an elaborate recording set-up by any means and the time I would normally put aside after a tour like that, to come back and write for the album, I didn't do anything. I remember having the recorder and barely turning the thing on. I was going through living hell. In the end, it worked out— I dispatched her back to Holland and we got divorced and then I sent my son to live in Wales with my mother and I went to record the album. So I didn't really have a lot to do with it."

"At the time, Neil had a big role," continues Tonka, summing up Carter in a more positive light. "At that point in time Neil was like a catalyst, the glue, in a lot of situations. Because he's very talented, when it comes to playing sax and keyboards and different things. I believe now he's taken up the cello as well, a multi-instrumentalist. But Neil and I were pretty tight."

"That one was with Gary Lyons and that was done in Switzerland," chimes in Phil, on the subject of this pastiche of an album. "Oh yeah, Gary would do a 48-hour mix, which I thought was a bit dubious. He would start mixing and he'd be in there morning until night, and that's always a bit worrying. I'm not knocking Gary, but it's a bit worrying when you have a 48-hour mix. That is another vague period. Most of the stuff that was done during the '80s, there was that '80s thing about it. There was an abundance. Everybody was going berserk. In actual fact, *No Place to Run* with George Martin was the last album we made that was level-footed. Apart from that everything else was a bit berserk. I can remember now one very vital fact about *Mechanix*: We stole Neil Carter's and Paul Chapman's firewood from their chalet in the Alps so they couldn't light a fire. That was the biggest drama. I remember Tonka going, 'You stole our fucking firewood, you bastard! I've been recording all night and I'm frozen!' I remember that argument."

Mechanix opens with "The Writer," a vignette of sorts, Phil entering the ego-diseased mind of a hack plying his trade for the scandal sheets. Phil ascribes to the character a certain power to make or break, but the underlying theme is that his purpose in life is quite pathetic. Tonka has said that the song in fact lampoons one or another of certain famous Sounds and Kerrang! journalists. The song is a solid riff rocker, menacing at mid-pace, a subtle synth wash as support, a synth solo preceding a solo from a Tonka oddly reminiscent of Joe Perry. Then there's the sax—again Aerosmith coming to mind—which gets a little too invasive, mimicking the riff. Was this all too much for Pete?

"Yeah, I'm not bad on 'The Writer,'" says Neil warily with respect to his sax work. "I'm a lot better saxophonist now. But I had never played it properly then, really. I really played it for the album, only because I can play clarinet. It's the same embouchure, the same way of playing, of blowing. But I hadn't really experimented with the saxophone much at all. Now I play constantly because it's part of what I do. So I've developed as a saxophonist in the last ten to fifteen years, quite unbelievably. I'm a different person now. But then... no, it's fine. And the single on *Wild, Willing*, 'Lonely Heart,' that sounds all right. Not wonderful, but it's okay. But yes, I like 'The Writer,' although we never managed to play it all that well live. I like 'Let It Rain.' But to be honest, not wishing to burst the bubble, but I do look back on it, and now I think some of it was a bit putting bits on bits to make it into a song, rather than actually thinking of it as a whole. I can see the flaws in some of them, but there's great energy there. I actually like a lot of the earlier UFO stuff myself, from before I joined the band. I think they really hold together well as songs more so than some of the stuff I did with them, anyway."

Next up was a cover of old lip-sneered chestnut "Somethin' Else," also then recently covered by fallen Sex Pistol Sid Vicious, who also, incidentally (coincidentally?) had covered "C'mon Everybody."

"I don't know; that was Pete's idea," says Tonka warily. "Even in Lone Star, we did the Beatles song, and it's a nice talking point, if you do a cover. 'Mystery Train' was the one from *No Place to Run*. And 'Somethin'

Else,' Eddie Cochran... I think Pete was going through an Eddie Cochran/Gene Vincent phase. He had a compilation tape at the time of all the people that had died in Britain who were like that (laughs). Johnny Kid & the Pirates, those kinds of people. I used to play the song before, in a local band, with that arrangement, which was a bit heavier; it was in a different key than the original and this kind of stuff."

"But the only problem with that was when Gary was, 'Oh, let's try this, let's try this.' It was Gary's idea to put the saxophone on it, and that's when Pete was going, 'That's fucking awful! You know, it should be a screaming guitar solo. It should be heavy and raw and gritty.' All of a sudden, we came in one day, and Gary had spent like three hours fixing a Mellotron, the tape-driven sampler affair with a keyboard. Somehow or other, the Mellotron ended up on there. I was like, 'What the hell is that doing there?!' I don't know. He obviously had a vision for how it should sound, different a bit from what we had."

So yes, again, probably more pronounced than anywhere on the album, was the sax. "No, he really didn't want it, "says Neil, of good ol' Pete. "Again, you look back on it—and we're talking twenty years ago—I look back and go, yeah, I suppose he had a point. He didn't like it and he didn't like the way things were going. He didn't particularly like our new manager, as well, at the time of *Mechanix*. I think he liked things the way they were before, if you know what I mean. There were a lot of things wrong. It's just a shame, really because he was great. Pete was a very good, sort of semi-front man, and he was the heart of the group really—well, he and Phil. I look back on it now, and I see the line-up changes, and it's unbelievable. I've heard they've just been out again. You know, I couldn't do it. I had the horrors looking at it, thinking, how can you keep doing this? But they obviously want to, and good power to them."

Mid-side, *Mechanix* offered up a very Springsteen-ish pop ballad called "Back into My Life," a requiem to squandered love and subsequent poignant self-reflection in the loneliness of a city street filled with life and lovers and sex—if not for the narrator. Despite multiple band protestations that there was no thought of or influence from Thin Lizzy, this is Phil Lynott all the way. Then again, perhaps both Phils had cast admiring eyes toward New Jersey's favourite son. Great song in any event, buttressed by big female backing vocals, and, thankfully, no sax. Issued as a single (backed with "The Writer") two months after the launch of the album, it sank like a rock without charting—even in the UK.

"Phil always had certain themes," reflects Neil. "There was the Springsteen thing; that comes into it a couple of times. I think he was keen on American street life. If you look at the lyrics, they do have that edge to them. His famous girlfriend Jean came into it quite a bit. He did used to read quite a lot of things. 'Profession of Violence' was the Krays thing. Always slightly dodgy thematic material, to do with gangsters and the street, gritty stuff; it did appeal to him."

But not Thin Lizzy? "Phil? I don't think so, no. Thin Lizzy and UFO, entirely different animals, really. If you actually look at the two groups, Thin Lizzy is almost like a different style of rock music—you've got that Celtic influence. You never get that with UFO, which is essentially British, a very British rock act, with American leanings. Because they spent a lot of time in America, there were slight Americanisms. But Thin Lizzy, not at all—very much not a British band. Phil Lynott was an Irishman, completely different, although I can't put it into words. But no, I don't remember any comments from Phil about Thin Lizzy. UFO were more so towards America and Americana."

Following "Back into My Life" was a menacing rocker—albeit one destined for obscurity—called "You'll Get Love." Dour, a bit flaccid, it's still got mood, providing a sort of adhesive to the album. Plus Paul's solo is gritty and streetwise, underscoring Phil's smouldering anger at a prospective love, or at least conquest, getting on with business a room away.

Closing side one is "Doing It All for You," a near classic that starts badly then picks up, building stature through a number of passages. Somewhat a heavy metal boogie, the song also contains a gorgeous melodic chorus and later on, an exquisite riff from Paul that is the highlight of the whole album. Phil turns in a colourful lyric sympathetic to the two-bit criminal going to work, stealing cars this particular early AM, to support himself and his bird.

A full-on, phase-shifted rocker called "We Belong to the Night" opens side two, for once, Gary Lyons' dirty production working in concert with the band's menacing stance and Phil's nocturnal street creature lyric, most of it to do with ladies of the night and their urge to break free from the cycle. Meat and potatoes all the way, Phil proves himself relentless in his street-tough themes, now well into his second full album of tart tales. "'We Belong to the Night' was another Lone Star one," says Paul. "It's called 'The Samurai' on the Lone Star one. The fast guitar to it, that intro, that was the Lone Star part, and then there's the middle part."

Neil indicates more of a collaborative vibe on the track, emphasizing the contrast between the haphazardness of UFO and the discipline of his later years with a successful run of Gary Moore albums.

"The riff to that one… what we used to do sometimes, is that we would come together with tapes of ideas and we would decide that, that bit I wrote went very well with that bit Paul wrote. So we would make a song of the bits and then put it together as a number. I used to do that with Gary Moore as well. He had something, I had something, and we would realise it would all work well together. So there were a lot of joint ventures, but it wasn't a case of sitting together and writing. We would write separately and then come together and say, well, that would actually work well with this, and we would tend to write as backing tracks. Then Phil would come to it and put something to it. So it was never written as a song, as such, which is slightly different to the way some people must write. I mean, Gary Moore would write with the song in mind and certainly, over the years I was with Gary, I would write whole songs. He may not use the entire song, but he would use elements of the song. So the UFO songs were written in a rather piecemeal fashion."

Contrasting what he wrote versus what might arise from Pete or Paul, Neil figures, "I tended to write in riffs; I tended to like quite hard riffs and Pete would come up with hard riffs as well. But then you need something to balance that. So there are the ballads. I can't remember how 'Terri' came to be at all, but it would tend to be chord sequences and things. Start to finish it was an evolving process, how the songs would get written and changed. Whereas, like I said, comparing it to Gary Moore, we would write almost complete songs before we even touched a studio. So you would actually write it at home on an eight-track or something so you'd have complete songs. So when you went into the studio, you actually weren't wasting any time. So it's all how you approach something. The song would actually be the song and you might actually play it as a song, before you actually approached the studio."

"Really, if you look back on it, particularly in this country, perhaps the world, this political correctness and the correctness of everyone behaving and watching the pennies and really thinking… Like I said, it was really only when I started with Gary Moore, and beforehand with UFO and Wild Horses, who were even worse. I mean, there were some terrible things in that band. But when I joined Gary's outfit, I could just see how professional people were. I don't count myself as among the wasters of the world and I used to think, well, that's just how people behave. Because I was very young, it was only really when I got with Gary that I saw how it could be done and therefore, you come out ahead of the game, instead of always in debt. It's just a philosophy of life. Gary is just so hyper-professional, it's only when you realise this, you say goodness me. With UFO, we never knew how much money we were spending. We had no idea; no one ever told us. We must have been spending shitloads of money to sort of write songs in a recording studio that was costing God knows what a day."

Back to *Mechanix*, next up was "Let It Rain," a bit of a hit for the band. In fact, the track was issued as an advance single, backed with non-LP track "Heel of a Stranger." A powerful popster, "Let It Rain" really got melodic come chorus time. Still, a snarling, guitar-charged break swung things back to the rock, all the while Phil getting inside the head of a woman caught up with a married man reluctant to leave his other, more stable life.

Says Paul of the dark side of the single, "'Heel of a Stranger'... when I heard that, I was like, 'Was that me? I can't even remember doing this track.' And they're like, 'It bloody was!' And it was one of the best ones; I don't know why it never went on the record! I listened to it and I was like, wow! I don't even know what it came out on. It was getting very mushy at that point." Tonka's right. This is a strong, melodic, radio-friendly b-side, if a bit pandering toward, say, a Bryan Adams direction. Come to think of it, the chorus is quite annoying, and its status as non-LP b-side ultimately seems appropriate.

"Terri" follows, UFO offering a true soppy, sappy ballad that somewhat works due to its mournful melodies and Phil's articulate, psychologically convincing lyric concerning fading romance. Offers Paul, "I know that Gary Lyons put the middle part of the song on there; he wrote it. He sat down at the piano and put these chords together, right before the solo. I think maybe Neil came up with a part of that. That's a hazy one."

For *Mechanix*, the string arrangements were Neil Carter's (note also Gary's assertion that he was involved), even if Neil now considers them a bit rudimentary.

"Again, with hindsight, having these people in... I had written an arrangement for 'Terri.' And having a string section in and obviously looking at this pathetic arrangement I had done and thinking, 'God what are we doing here? But we're getting paid.' I mean, things like that. And finishing the album off at six in the morning—ridiculous—Phil and

Gary and I sitting around and finishing this album off, because it had to be done at a certain point, with all the time that had been wasted in the past. Suddenly you're rushing to get it finished."

"But UFO, they were a good, typical band of that era," reflects Carter. "There were sort of the brilliant bits; it's a great feeling, when you're playing live and things are working. You know, headlining at Reading with them, my first concert, fantastic; it really was, because they had built quite a reputation at that point. But unfortunately, they were their own worst enemies. It's a shame, a great shame. They were a good band, but they could've been a really great band. But yes, my string arrangements are on there. I think there were some very, very good ones on *The Wild, the Willing and the Innocent* (credited to Paul Buckmaster). Unfortunately the ones I did were fairly basic (laughs). I could probably manage it better now, but then I had been a bit out of the loop sort of writing music and scoring for so long, I had just forgotten what to do. I was only asked to do it because there was no one else to do it. Again... playing with a new toy."

Mechanix closes strongly with two rockers, the first being "Feel It," the final track on the record being "Dreaming." "Feel It" is credited to Way/Mogg, and the riff is old-time meat and potatoes "Louie Louie"/AC/DC all the way, pure Pete, with UFO's usual sense of class and melody come break and chorus time, Phil turning in a (sub?) standard tale of mischievous womanly seduction.

"'Dreaming' was more of a Neil thing," says Paul of the combative fastback heavy metal rocker closing out *Mechanix*. "I really love the song. If you listen to the last thing, it has the layered vocals, with Neil doing the left and right stereo: 'dreaming.' One is carrying on while one is coming over the top."

Indeed, the track is credited to Carter/Mogg, again demonstrating the bench strength of the band, the versatility of the writing, the fortuitous situation that had the keyboardist writing non-keyboard-like hard rockers—because as with Paul Raymond, the keyboardist could think like a guitarist as well. As Chapman alludes to, the song closes with a nice layered vocal arrangement that comes off almost as a classic "round." Phil's lyric is quintessential Mogg, a tale of petty teenage gang life in Brighton hormonally befuddled with a sense of another, only slightly more respectable purpose in life, delivered by the enthralling, life-altering example of a rock 'n' roll band heard, poetically, through the floor and the stage door, membranes that, in a flash, seemed less impermeable—dreams could, in fact, come true.

Concurrent with the release of *Mechanix* was a double live album from the Michael Schenker Group. *One Night at Budokan* has seen a miniature version of what *Strangers in the Night* has gone through over the years, namely, a steady, resolute, press-fuelled rise to status as a great live album. Indeed, the songs from the first two MSG studio records could only improve with respect to delivery, and some might even say overall sonics—they are "freed" here, beyond their cloistered capture on two aseptic studio records. Included on Michael's record is a rendition of "Doctor Doctor."

Out on the UFO tour, Neil Carter upheld the fine tradition forged by Paul Raymond, namely playing lots of guitar and surprisingly little keyboards. "I always hated being chained to the keyboards," says Neil. "As I got on a bit more and started to get more confident onstage, I actually preferred playing the guitar. When I look at myself—because I've got loads of videos from back then—and I look at the way I am with UFO, when I first joined them, I look like this little mousy creature. And then I could obviously see my confidence grow, especially when I was with Gary. I look at things like the Ice Stadium. There's a video of us in Stockholm and I'm a completely different person to the person I see with UFO. But I didn't like being chained to the keyboards. I liked playing guitar."

Asked whether he was a good guitarist, Neil says, "No, I'm a dreadful guitarist, actually. I mean, I'm a rhythm guitarist, basically; that's what I do. I couldn't play lead. And the more the years went on, the more I realised that I'm not a lead player. With Gary, I wouldn't even attempt to play any leads (laughs). I used to do tiny bits with Paul. But I would actually say I'm quite a good rhythm guitarist. I think that's what I do well."

The *Mechanix* tracks that did well live were essentially "We Belong to the Night" and "Let It Rain," both lasting into the tour for the next album. "Terri" and "Doing It All for You" were also played. As a side note, "Long Gone," "Makin' Moves" and "The Wild, the Willing and the Innocent" from the record of the same name also lasted through most of the Paul Chapman era.

"Well, er, um, I suppose riled-up is the word," says Neil, on the subject of Phil and his supposed violent streak, a topic that comes up invariably when addressing the tour trail. "It's very much an English expression: very riled-up. Perturbed is I think the word. But with certain people, it's always alcohol-related, fuelled by too much drink. You see it on a daily basis. People in clubs and pubs where I live here. So in a rock environment, in a charged environment, you know, you come off stage and something could always happen. He did have his moments and to me, I can't stand it. But so be it. It doesn't really matter in the grand scheme of things. But definitely there are moments I would rather forget. Put it that way."

And what of the band's famous love of pranks? "Yeah, I mean, they were always directed against Andy. It's all very childish stuff. It's like nicking things. Or you would go to a Holiday Inn in those days, and they would have some convention, so they would go and nick all the letters and make up things for Andy. I don't know, just constant jokes about Andy and his wife. I think they regarded me as this little saintly figure who would do no harm to anyone. My wife and I would be on tour, and just to get away from them—because to be honest, sometimes they were a bit much—we'd go sit at the back of the tour bus. They'd call it The Chapel, because my ex-wife and I used to sit there just trying to escape them (laughs). But it's funny, watching Monty Python a lot, a tremendous amount. Doing sort of more interesting substances than was good for them and drinking rather a lot. I mean, just daft things. Obviously, now, I get so tired these days, I'm in bed by 10:00. But back then, staying up for three days. You know what rock bands were like in those days. It's nothing that Mötley Crüe haven't done ten times over, or anyone else. They tend to stick to a pattern, I think (laughs)."

September 1982 saw Pete Way's name crop up on the back of Twisted Sister's blistering debut album *Under the Blade*, as producer. Says Twisted Sister guitarist J.J. French, "It was an exciting experience to finally get the chance to make a record after struggling for ten years. Pete produced it, and you know, he did not do much producing. It was primitive but it was fine. He was drinking a lot at the time, so Mark Mendoza ended up producing a lot of it. But it was a fun experience. We recorded it on a mobile truck in a barn in southern England, and the amplifiers were separated by hay bales. I remember that. I remember the farmer said that his chickens laid 30% more eggs when Mendoza did his basic tracks."

If 1982 was the year for a bit of a wobbler from UFO, it was also the year for what is – in this writer's opinion the finest album discussed in this book from anybody within the UFO orbit to UFO itself. That record is *Assault Attack*, the third studio album from the Michael Schenker Group, issued in October of '82 and given its beyond classic qualities, the story bears some detailed telling. Call this a lengthy digression if you will (and please accept my apology), but I do certainly believe

Assault Attack is better than any UFO record ever made (and by the way, we've got another fine, fine UFO-associated album to chat about in a bit of detail further down the line).

For *Assault Attack*, Schenker acquires ex-Rainbow belter Graham Bonnet and Deep Purple studio legend Martin Birch to provide a one-two punch that would make the record impressively explosive.

"He's a very talented guy," muses Graham Bonnet on producer Martin Birch. "It was the first time I had met him and it was the last time I ever saw him. I was at his house for awhile when we were doing the album, because we had to do a lot of the old songs for live gigs; I had to listen to all the old Michael Schenker albums. Martin is a very good producer and a very musical guy; I got on with him very well. We had a lot of fun messing around in the studio, probably too much time wasted with silly English songs, instead of getting on with the recording. He would go, 'Oh, can I come and sing that with you, Graham?' But eventually we got through it. But after that he went with one band, signed up with them to record with them and nobody else. They said, we want you exclusively to be our producer and not go anywhere else. That was the story I heard. Whether it's true or not, I don't know." That exclusive client would appear to be Iron Maiden, for which the man known for knob-jobbing heavy classics for the likes of Deep Purple, Black Sabbath and Blue Öyster Cult, would work with through that band's *Fear of the Dark* before retiring.

But before we get to production, a change of drummers would take place. "That was one argumentative afternoon in London when we were rehearsing," recalls Bonnet of that fateful day when the very opinionated Cozy Powell would be ousted. "Something happened, I don't know, I wasn't there. They were rehearsing and there was an argument between Cozy and Michael. Drumsticks were flying and whatever else and he upset Michael very, very badly. Michael ended up in tears. I remember being told by some of the guys, who said, 'Michael is crying; he's so upset about it.' And Michael said, 'I can't work with you anymore, Cozy.' And that's when Ted McKenna (Sensational Alex Harvey Band, Rory Gallagher) came in. It wasn't because Cozy wasn't playing good or anything like that. It had nothing to do with his talent, because the guy is brilliant. It was just a personal conflict between the two of them."

"We all lived in this house in London when we were making that album," continues Bonnet, "all of us together, Ted, Michael Schenker, Chris Glen (note: also a SAHB alumnus), the bass player, and I. We all lived in this house with a couple of the roadies. It was unbearable. Every day would turn into an argument because we all got on top of each other. Everybody was up at different hours of the day and it was a stressful time."

Michael, in his inimitable cut-and-paste manner, sums up the writing of the album this way. "They were all just written at the same time. That whole album was done at the rehearsal studio. I actually had an argument with my girlfriend, and I moved into the rehearsal room and I would sleep there and write, sleep and write, sleep and write until it was done. So it was basically all about that. When it was done, then the singer came in and it was done from there."

"Michael's a very private person, I know that," ventures Bonnet, when asked to provide a psychological profile of the enigmatic Mr. Schenker. "I know that if I would go into the room when he was getting stuff together with his guitar, he wouldn't hardly talk. He'd always be miles away in another world; I remember that. And most of the time totally on his own—he's very much a loner—or with his girlfriend at the time. Because that was what was happening and he was very much into her. Apart from being in the studio, I never really saw him very much. It was just basically when we were recorded and going through ideas for songs. As I said, I think he's a very private person. He's got his own mind. Sometimes he's hard to understand, probably because he's a Kraut (laughs). Because he's German. He has a different way of looking at things. He says, 'I'm very serious about this.' Yes, he's very serious. Sometimes Cozy and I would make jokes, and he wouldn't get them. But as I said, he seems very private. He thinks a lot."

Another stumbling block with respect to constructing this third MSG album was the perhaps overlooked fact that "the singer" had never written lyrics, or indeed melodies before. I say overlooked, because the following comment from Michael seems to indicate he thought that Bonnet was up to his elbows in the writing of Rainbow's *Down to Earth*. Not true, as Roger Glover had done all that previous to recording, not to mention having auditioned around eighty singers for the tough Rainbow post.

"I don't know what happened with Graham," is Schenker's bemused, but not derogatory summation of events more than twenty years after the fact. "I don't know how he was writing songs with Ritchie Blackmore. I don't know what is different. But when he was in my surroundings, when we worked together, he was kind of unusual. He was almost like shy or embarrassed to come up with anything; it was very strange. I'm not much of an outgoing person myself, I'm pretty shy myself, so having two shy people sitting there, not knowing what to do..."

"But I kind of started to get into his frame of mind, to try to loosen things up. It was the most unusual situation (laughs). I don't even know if I should talk about it. I think I have in the past. He just needed... you know when you get into new situation, and people kind of feel that the ice is not broken? I guess maybe my music was written already and I confronted him and put him on the spot. Maybe that's the way to put it. Maybe he was put on the spot. Because I had everything ready, and now I put the tape on to tell him to do something with it, and maybe I would have liked to do it myself, to be honest, if I think about it now. Basically I was expecting him to come up with something for me, which is an unusual thing in itself. Yet he did, finally. He came up with stuff. But he couldn't make up words; he wasn't comfortable with just improvising words, just for the sake of finding melodies, for the riffs that I was writing and so on. So I suggested to him, just pick up this magazine and read something out of it and that made it for him. He used it as a tool, and at that moment, he went bang, bang, bang. So I guess it was a good thing in a way."

An accurate depiction from Herr Schenker? "I don't know; I can't remember," answers Graham. "I just know he was a bit worried about getting it all going because as I said, he didn't know how to write any lyrics in good English. And when I did finish, I know he was very pleased with what I did, what I came up with in the end. It turned out okay."

Backing up, Graham tells the tale from his side of things. "Well, it was something I had never done! With Rainbow, for instance, everything was... apart from some of the melodies, all of the words were made up by Roger Glover. He wrote all the lyrics. I had never really done any songwriting as such. I remember one day rehearsing with Michael and he said to me (in a German accent), 'You have to write some words, Graham. I don't speak English very good and I can't write words very well. And you have to come up with melodies.' I said, 'You show me where the things go and I'll try my best.' So I just sat down for a few weeks and it was a learning experience, to try and do words."

"Because as I said, I had never tried it. All the songs I had recorded in the past were written by other people, such as The Bee Gees in '68, etc., so I basically would just go to the studio and sing the song. Whereas now, I had to put the song together. It was a bit of a puzzle because a lot of the arrangements were very long. Some of the songs went on for like ten minutes and I'm going, well, where the hell does the verse go?! You know, there's a lot of guitar playing (laughs). Where do I fit my bit in? So I had to go through things with him. We had to edit a lot of the songs down, because we would just keep playing and come up with a new bit for a new song. And like I said, sometimes ten, fifteen minutes long, twenty minutes long, and so we'd have to edit them down."

"I think Cozy helped with that," continues Bonnet. "He would say, 'This is way too long, Michael; where is Graham going to do anything on these tracks?' So Cozy helped cut them down so I could fit in my words. I just sat down with a newspaper or something, to try to find a subject, or magazine, just to get a subject for a song. Because I didn't know where to start. Then after awhile I thought, oh wait a minute, I don't need to sit with a newspaper, it just came. I thank Michael for that, for forcing me to try something I'd never done before, which I didn't really think I could do very well."

After the communal experience in London, the band was off—with Ted McKenna, not Cozy—to pastoral France to begin recording. "This is something I could never understand," laughs Bonnet. "People always want to go to remote haunted mansions to make albums. You end up being really bored and not knowing what to do. There's a little village nearby with about twelve people living in it. Everybody thinks it's good to have loneliness and quiet, to compose music and record. But I find the opposite. I need a break to go into a city, and go around the stores or something. After awhile we all became like that, in France. It got like, well, what are we going to do today? We're going to go down to the local little bar and sit there all afternoon. So what happened was, we went to Munich, to the city, and we recorded the rest of the album actually in a city setting, which is much better because you could get out and see people, rather than just each other all day."

As an aside (from our aside!), I wanted to clear the rumour I had heard in a few places that Graham performed his vocals in his God-given birthday suit, no bonnet, no nothing.

"No (laughs). If I did, I can't remember. I usually take my shirt off. That is one thing I do do, and undo my trousers. Because you can breathe a little bit more with your fly open (laughs). That's probably about as far as I got. They might have fallen down once or twice; I don't know. I guess stories get exaggerated a little bit. But I would always take my shirt off, because I would get hot or whatever. Yeah, I like to be relaxed, but probably not that relaxed (laughs)."

"No," exclaims Schenker, with a laugh, when asked if *Assault Attack*'s lead single, the shamelessly poppy "Dancer" was written to be a hit single. "I mean, never, ever have I written a song looking for a hit single. Never, ever in my life. I wouldn't even know how to do that because I'm not an expert in writing for singles and I don't even know what it takes to write one. But it was just one of those riffs that was there, and it just turned out to be a little more memorable and commercial than any of the others."

Michael indicated that I would have to ask Graham if the lyrics were directed that way, and after a pretty emphatic yes, Bonnet goes on to explain the song's lyric.

"'Dancer' was basically... that was one where I *did* read the newspaper. I read a newspaper article about Toni Basil, the choreographer. It's about her, basically. I met her back in the '70s when she was working with Muhammad Ali, Cassius Clay, as he originally was, and she had a group of dancers called The Lockers. I came to America with a girlfriend of mine and she was doing this show called *Lampoon*, which in fact, got cancelled because the magazine said you can't use our name. The magazine people were going to sue if the show went on the air. That's when I met her and I thought gee, these guys are great dancers and I talked to her a bit, and she had worked with David Bowie. And Muhammad Ali, he was boxing and these dancers would go into the ring and dance with her. So I thought, what an interesting person. We talked for a long time and I saw this article about her and later on she made a record, which was that 'Mickey' record and it's kinda funny. So I wrote that about her."

But if "Dancer" was this record's somewhat rankling "Since You Been Gone," it is side two opener "Desert Song" that is considered the album's classic. Graham's band still plays it live, and besides "Dancer," it is one of his favourites of the album, his thinking aligning with that of the fans.

"'The Desert Song' tune was the first lyric I wrote; in about ten minutes, I think. Because it was written in the rehearsal room. I remember Michael saying to me, 'We don't have any words to this. Just write anything.' I just started to wander off into this thing about being in the desert; camels and all the rest of it (laughs). I just drifted off into my own little world and we came up with that, that evening, rehearsing. But it's basically about people going through the desert on camels. It was a silly thing. It was kind of like, add water, and there's your lyrics."

"I still like 'Assault Attack' very much, but people always come up with 'Desert Song,'" notes Michael, agreeing that this one is a fan favourite. "I was never too keen with the vocals on 'Desert Song.' It was too dragging for my liking. But people keep coming up to me and saying, 'Desert Song,' 'Desert Song.' But for myself it was 'Assault Attack.'"

Michael is also a fan of the album's instrumental, "Ulcer." "Yes, I like that instrumental very much, which was supposed to be a vocal song. It was kept to do at the last moment, and Graham did not know what to do with it. He had absolutely no idea. So Martin said, 'We have a song, but we can't make a song with vocals, so we have to turn it into an instrumental.' So I went up into my hotel room and it was already the mixing period. So in one afternoon I created that instrumental, and it just turned out to be one of my favourite instrumentals. I can't really even play it live because I find it too difficult to perform live to get it as good as I did it on the record. Because it has the double bass drum and it has lots of overdubs on it. I feel that live, I either want it the way it was on the record or not at all."

"Rock You to the Ground" is another highlight of the record, with its hefty heavy metal stripper vibe. It's bluesy, but more so, it's metal. Graham is manic on it, putting in a powerful vocal that seethes with passion. "It was just a basic rock tune," recalls Graham. "No particular influence. I just started writing and stuff came out that sounded right with the melody. It sounded tough. Use tough words. If it means nothing, use words that sound tough (laughs). That's what I remember about that."

Elsewhere, "Broken Promises" pulses slowly but muscularly to a rock-solid Chris Glen bass line. "Searching for a Reason" works off a bit of a gallop, but the melody is both poppy and mournful at once, very Rainbow-like. Maybe the album's heaviest track is "Samurai," an even more Rainbow-like track than "Searching for a Reason," given the former's sweeping gothic melody.

In closing, Graham expresses fondness for the record. "I'm very proud of that album. The tracks are very different from each other. I like the way Michael plays. He's a very different composer; he's got a very unique style. He's not like your regular so-called heavy metal guitar player."

"Chris Glenn, very solid," offers Michael, summing up the quality of the album's short-lived line-up. "Ted McKenna, a little bit more jazzy at times, but also he can be very solid. He was very good on that *Assault*

Attack album, and Martin Birch was very good with his production. Actually it was the most liked album when it comes down to the opinion of musicians. Most musicians like *Assault Attack* better than any other MSG albums, vocally, in terms of the guitar playing, production, everything."

Post-album came touring. Or did it? For this hopeful, well-regarded line-up, it was emphatically not to be. Incredibly, Graham would not last a single gig with the band.

"That was a terrible day," recalls Bonnet with a palpable shudder. "I'll never forget it, and nobody else will either (laughs). It was one very stupid afternoon in the pub and then having a bit too much of this and a bit too much of that. Michael was doing some stuff as well (laughs). There was an argument in the dressing room before we did the show. He wouldn't let me in to get some stuff I wanted. He had my jacket in there or something silly. 'Fucking let me in! Let me in. I want to get my clothes out, you know?' He said no, piss off. 'Oh, okay.'"

"This was just before the gig and so, I just got pretty loaded, to be honest with you. It was a stupid mistake, which I hope I never do again. It was awful, just dreadful. I had all these songs to sing, which I didn't know very well. I had put them all out on pieces of paper—old Michael Schenker stuff—all along the front of the stage and the crowd pushed forward, and all the papers were scattered and it just screwed me up. I didn't know what I was doing. I didn't know where I was or anything. It was bad. Because we were supposed to do the Castle Donington gig a few days later. I apologized to them profusely. I was like, 'Oh God, I'm really sorry.' And they reckoned that I couldn't do the gig that was coming up, the Monsters of Rock thing. I'm like, 'No, I can do it!' And my manager said, 'No, they've fired you. You've got to go back to Los Angeles.' And that's what I did. It was horrible. It was an awful time."

Back in UFO's world, there were problems on the road as well, especially during the waning days of the Paul Chapman era. Live the band had its good nights and its bad nights, due to drugs and fatigue.

"Most nights, Phil had this terrible frustration, because he knew he wasn't performing as well as he might," reflects Andy Parker. "Because it really upset him that his voice was shot and that can really make a lot of difference. Of course, you come onstage and not having a good show, you get into this horrible post-mortem that would always end up in arguments. 'You fucked up.' 'What, you think I fucked up?! You fucked up worse than me.' To be honest, I used to be so exhausted when I came offstage, I was trying doubly hardly to keep it together. I used to just try to and avoid getting involved in the post-mortem. Because you can bet your life it would happen every night, that someone would get upset. But the studio was different. Because there's not that pressure being out in front of thousands of people and making a fool of yourself. But believe you me, we were spending too much money and time in the studio—all the time."

Chapter Four
Making Contact

"If that's the way you feel, let's go right now!"

Fragile, spent and on their last legs, our bloodied heroes surprised fans by chiming in with a tough, accomplished, cohesive record for 1983 called *Making Contact*. But founding member Pete Way would be gone by this point, off to form Fastway, and then, after an aborted liaison with Ozzy, Waysted.

Said Pete on leaving UFO, "I just think you tour and tour and tour and you basically get to a point where you want to get away from the ever-revolving thing and want to try something else. There was also tension in the band and we didn't have a break at all. After I left, it did virtually break up. It was an inevitable thing because I don't think you can work quite that much. A bit of brain damage in the end, you know?"

Pete's stay in his namesake Fastway, along side Motörhead's Fast Eddie Clarke and fresh Irish belter Dave King would be short-lived due to contractual hassles and other less discussed factors. When the band's classic self-titled debut record was launched in March of '83, Pete was nowhere to be seen.

On the press trail for the first album with Waysted, *Vices*, Pete ran through the gnashing of teeth that took him through the end of UFO, then Ozzy, then Fastway. "I get exhausted just thinking about everything that's happened. But everything's turned out very well. I'm happy with this band, and the experiences I went through before getting here have reinforced my commitment to this group. I spent enough time listening to other people tell me what to do. Now I have a band where everyone knows what to do without even being told."

"I'm really not that hard to get along with," continued Pate. "There were things going on in all those bands that forced my hand. The situation with UFO was totally intolerable. We were once a great hard rock band. What was happening though was that we were becoming too soft. I didn't want that at all. I'm a rocker. I'll stay that way 'til the bitter end. That's why I jumped at the opportunity to tour with Ozzy. I felt that if nothing else, I would be able to get on stage and play some real rock 'n' roll again. Ozzy's a good bloke, but he does have a very set way of playing. He doesn't like you to vary what you're doing very much. We both knew that my time in his band would be limited, and I view that experience very positively. I can't say the same about Fastway. At first Eddie and I saw eye to eye on the direction that band should be headed. Suffice to say that after a short time, we didn't see eye to eye anymore."

"I was in a little band in Dublin and we had done a demo," explains King on securing the Fastway gig. "We were called Stilwood. Literally I got the gig from just reading the music magazines back home. Eddie and Pete Way just started to get this band together and they wanted a lead singer and they wanted somebody new. I sent a demo tape that I had made with Stilwood and I guess I got the gig."

As mentioned, shortly thereafter, Pete Way would flee the band for what he thought would be greener pastures. Micky Feat, a friend of Fastway drummer Jerry Shirley, would ultimately play bass on that excellent first album, but not be credited as a band member.

"Yeah, Pete had gotten the call to do Ozzy's British tour," says Dave. "And I think Pete was under the impression he was going to get the whole thing, but it didn't work out that way. Then Pete felt very bad about leaving the whole situation. Pete's a lovely guy. Pete contributed a couple of months as far as I remember (laughs). We got the record deal when Pete was in the band but then he got the Ozzy thing. I always loved Pete's energy and his enthusiasm. He's a good guy to be around and he helped us write 'Feel Me, Touch Me,' maybe 'Easy Livin'' and 'All I Need Is Your Love.' After that, I think nothing else as far as I can remember."

In a parallel surreal world, both Pete and a guitarist by the name of Michael Schenker might have ended up in Ozzy's band. "I got the phone call in the middle of the night from a very nervous Ozzy Osbourne," recalls Schenker. "Randy had just crashed in the plane. I guess I was his first choice because I was one of Randy's favourite guitarists. He must have talked about me because Ozzy called me up. I am glad I didn't end up doing it because I guess he was dragging people across the stage and pulling them by the hair and stuff like that. I have thin hair and

And so the Tonka era begins: Paul Raymond (left) and Paul Chapman (right), De Montfort Hall, Leicester, February 5th, 1979.
(© Alan Perry)

Pete Way, there through thick and thin, second in loyal membership only to Phil himself.
(© Alan Perry)

Phil: "He did it."
(© Alan Perry)

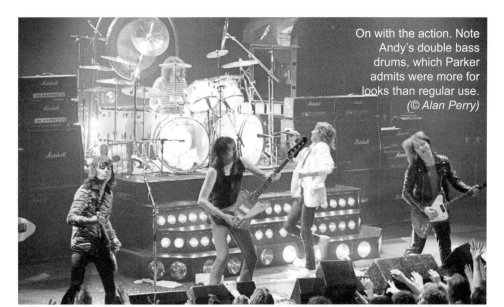
On with the action. Note Andy's double bass drums, which Parker admits were more for looks than regular use. *(© Alan Perry)*

Paul Chapman,
January 27, 1980
at the Coventry Theatre.
(© Alan Perry)

More shots from the band's Coventry Theatre
No Place to Run tour date.
(© Alan Perry)

UFO referee and amused observer Andy Parker. *(© Alan Perry)*

Misdemeanor era record label promo photo. Left to right: Paul Raymond, Paul Gray, Phil Mogg, Jim Simpson, Tommy "Atomik Tommy M" McClendon.

You can't say that Chrysalis didn't throw any ad money behind *Misdemeanor*.

Michael Schenker with his preferred solo band singer in the late '80s, Robin McAuley, plus ad for "Anytime" from 1989's *Save Yourself*.

Tongue in cheek Japanese ad for the *Walk on Water* reunion album.

Michael, with beard, in a label promo shot that accompanied the *Written in the Sand* album, his solo project directly following his time with UFO for *Walk on Water*.

Paul Raymond, Michael Schenker and Phil Mogg in the 2010s. Phil has expressed a desire to retire, but Michael never tires. *(Courtesy of Bill Baran)* there would not have been much left if I had joined him! I always liked Ozzy. I think he has a unique voice. It's not a technical voice but you can really identify it. Who knows what would have happened to him if I had joined? Who knows what would have happened to Whitesnake or Aerosmith if I had joined them?"

"If you are happy with your current situation or you at least know where you are at this particular moment then you are okay," reflects Michael. "You don't have any idea where you would be if you had done something else. If you are pretty happy with your present time then you can be grateful, even with the ups and downs. It is like my brother says all the time, 'No energy gets lost in the universe.' We are going through a journey with lots of lessons to learn. If we are fortunate enough and have the wisdom then we pick what we want to do in life. Some people have dreams when they are little but they lose their dreams due to competition and wanting to own a house and this and that. With myself, I was always more happy doing artistic things. I loved being creative playing guitar and drums. I had to learn to meditate and to learn to deal with my shyness. When people talk about me being a madmen and stuff like this, it basically comes down to numbing yourself from being shy and turning into the opposite."

In addition to the Ozzy offer, Michael mentions Whitesnake and Aerosmith, but by '84, Phil Lynott and Thin Lizzy were also bandied about as bandmates. "I remember that Phil had called me up and asked me to join his band. It was in '84. I don't know what happened. I was actually approached by various different ones in that same year. I think it was Whitesnake, Phil Lynott, Ian Hunter, and I said no to all of them. Ozzy was earlier. I've been approached by lots of people, but in that particular year, it was all in one moment, that I was approached by those three different bands. I don't usually mention them. It just so happens that I remember (laughs)."

Meanwhile Pete Way is not credited anywhere on the Fastway album. Here's Pete's remembrance on his brief Fastway experience, beginning with the song credit situation. "Actually, the choice was made for me. Basically Chrysalis Records stopped me from signing with CBS because there are clauses and such that said I was one of the main members of UFO. And actually, they wanted to sign Fastway but we had already made a deal with CBS and we got into that fight. You get into a position where you tour and tour and tour and you put something together that you thought was pretty good and then suddenly you're faced with court cases; it's difficult to take."

"On the other hand, it gave me the opportunity to do Waysted. I co-wrote everything on there with Eddie but I didn't get credit for it because I just handed it over. It was basically, 'You guys may as well take credit for it.' It was only fair. And there wasn't much of a choice really. I went and started Waysted, and I figured the boys would have to finish it off. But we basically credited everybody. That was the way we did it in rehearsal together. Some of it was coming out of jamming—not so much jamming because we knew what we were going to do—but putting different ideas together. We wanted it to be pretty much what it sounded like: Dave King singing raw, and I didn't want ballads, but a bit Zeppelin-ish, pretty much exactly the way the first album sounded."

So no Pete there, and no Pete in UFO, but by September of '83, nine months after the issue of *Making Contact*, Pete had another barnstormer of a record in the hot and heavy Waysted debut, perhaps a record even better than the under-rated, somehow under-stated UFO record of the same year.

"I've been involved with a lot of music in my life," said Pete at the time, to Hit Parader's Andy Secher, "but I haven't been this excited over a project in years. There's a satisfaction involved with putting a band together and watching it grow. Nothing else can match it. The band came together rather easily. And once we started rehearsing, I knew we had what I was looking for. There was a lot of energy in the music. To me, that was the most important thing. After seeing the way UFO degenerated toward the end, I thought it was essential to make music that had that spark of excitement again. I can't wait until we get on the road to show everyone what the songs sound like live. I've always believed that rock 'n' roll only sounds great when it's played on stage, and this band's ultimate proof of that. I'm quite pleased with the album, but let me warn everyone that the live show is going to be lethal!"

Back to the band at hand, one of the keys to *Making Contact* a success was in its disciplined, professional production at the hands of Mick Glossop, brought in to save what was going to be another Gary Lyons job. It was Chapman that brought out the axe.

"Gary Lyons and myself... it was an unusual situation, because he engineered the first Lone Star album, produced the second one, and then he did *Mechanix*, and he was going to do *Making Contact*. He had actually started doing it, and we fired him off the project. I was the one who had to tell him because I was the only one who had made three records with him (laughs). Everyone was saying, 'Well, you know him best. You've known him all these years.' That's all the more reason why I shouldn't have to do it! That was weird, how that worked out. So Mick Glossop did the record, and it turned out pretty cool."

Elaborating, Paul adds that, "when we were making *Making Contact*, Neil and I played most of the parts. I was going to play all the bass on *Making Contact*, but Neil pitched in a bit. But when we were making that, because Pete wasn't there, Chrysalis wanted Gary to do the album. I mean it was still a little bit... nobody was really gun-shy from the *Mechanix* thing. Because *Mechanix* did pretty well. We were touring America and everything. So the label thought, 'This is selling well, let's get him again.' So by this point Gary is divorced, and we went to The Manor; we were writing most of the stuff before we went there, and it was an expensive studio. All the studios we used were expensive, but The Manor was a little bit more expensive than most. It was Richard Branson's studio in Oxford. We were there for a week before Gary actually came out of his bedroom, upstairs with some hooker and leaning out the window. He had brought his own engineer from New York."

"And I said, 'This is a waste of time.' Gary just had no input. This guy was supposed to be taking control of the whole thing. So to cut a long story short, I was delegated, because this was the fourth album I was doing with Gary, whereas for everyone else it was their second. Because I knew him, I went and had a talk with him, and he said, 'If that's the way you feel, let's go right now!' He was so fucking defensive about it. We were only trying to communicate here. So to cut a long story short, we fired him. So Mick Glossop came in and took over and he had just finished doing a Van Morrison album or something like this and he was available and we retrieved the album from the very depths of midrange (laughs)."

"Indeed we had to fire Gary in the middle of it," recalls Andy. "He wasn't even coming down to the studio. We had to get rid of him. It was sad. The Manor is a big studio outside of Oxford, a big old manor house, and the studio was in a separate building. Gary was in this bedroom upstairs and he never came out! He was up there with his girlfriend. He never came down. 'Well, leave the studio door open or the window; I can hear from up here,' kind of thing and we thought, 'Look, this has gone far enough.'"

"Paul was elected to fire him, because Paul knew him best, because he was a mate of his! We had all got friendly with the guy. But the funny thing was, he'd just been down to the sweet shop, and brought back all these packets of sweets and stuff. Gary was just like a big kid all the time. He could just get out of order all the time. A little of him went a long way."

"For example," continues Andy, "I remember when we were doing *Mechanix* in Switzerland, and Queen had their studio in Montreux. We had dinner one night, and I came back from the toilet and my jacket was gone. There was giggling, 'Come on, where's my jacket?' But the thing was, he had thrown it out the window. And unfortunately for me it was out laying on the sidewalk out there. With my wallet and my green card and everything. He hadn't bothered to check. He just took it and flung it out the window. That's something Gary would do. If someone would have walked by and picked it up, it would've been gone. I was lucky that someone told me where it was and I went out there and it was still laying there. But that's the kind of thing he would do. So sometimes he would get really annoying."

"But yeah, he'd been down to the sweet shop and just bought a pile of sweets: 'Come here and see what I got.' And it really fell to Paul, because Paul had the longest history with him; he was nearer to him than anyone else. It was just getting to the point where is it was absurd and he was expensive. He wasn't a cheap producer to have, and he just wasn't doing his job, and we couldn't see it getting any better. So that's when they brought Mick Glossop in. But to be honest, Mick Glossop just kind of... Phil and Paul did that with Mick Glossop—it was a rescue job."

"We were really burned-out," sighs Paul. "When I say burned-out, it was from a physical touring point of view; we hadn't had time off for years. I mean, it's like trying to squeeze fifteen months out of every year. And it's pretty high pressure. The travelling alone, the actual physical distances, without the stress and musical and the family stuff... Everyone was going through divorces on *Making Contact*."

"And we all... except for Neil and Andy, actually that leaves me and Phil (laughs), we were pretty dependent on certain substances. Without a bass player of course, I'm taking on another role here and I actually really enjoyed making it, once Gary was out of the picture. That was when digital stuff started creeping in, digital keyboards and digital signal processors, so sounds were easier to get. Only it was a novel thing. It was the start of the downfall of the decline of creativity in studio situations. For example, on *The Good, the Bad, the Waysted*, on the track 'Manuel,' there's a stereo acoustic at the beginning, going 'dong' like a bell, and to create stereo, what I had to do was I had to put a mic in the corridor, one side of the corridor and a mic on the other side, and I had to tune the guitar, the open note, and I would bang the note and wave it between the two mics, just hold it up there and moving it, panning the mic left and right so you get a true stereo. That now would be simulated by a machine, see what I mean?"

"If I'm not mistaken, we did *Making Contact* in four studios, and every time you change studios you have to redo everything, and then you've got to go on the road and it's not quite ready, and we have no bass player, and that's when I called up Billy Sheehan, and Billy was like 'Yeah man! I'll do it! Great!' We were actually rehearsing for the tour and finishing the album at the same time."

"But from an overall point of view, after *Mechanix*, it was like a breath of fresh air for me. Some of the *Making Contact* songs were Neil-related, but the ones like 'Blinded by a Lie' and others, came out good. Plus there are a few also-rans that never made it onto the album, which have now since surfaced. There's a whole new Japanese thing that came out with all the obscurities on it. Plus at the time we weren't very responsive to remembering things anyway because of the condition we were in. But overall, I thought that was the best album we'd done for a long time. It's a shame that the band was to break up."

"Hmm... Gary Lyons, interesting character," adds the ever-diplomatic Neil Carter. "We did make *Mechanix* with him. He was quite good. But he was appalled by the fact that we hadn't had anything written by the time he had come to produce it. There was actually nothing to produce. But he's a very rock 'n' roll producer. He came to do *Making Contact* but he and us parted ways after about a week-and-a-half because he spent most of the time in bed. We ended up having Mick Glossop come in to finish up *Making Contact*, because Gary Lyons and us didn't really hit it off the second time. Mick Glossop was brilliant, very, very good indeed. But Gary... interesting character; and of course he had lots of stories because he'd worked with Queen and people like that. So I found that quite fascinating."

Back to Glossop, Carter opines that, "The best thing was that he actually thought along the same lines as particularly Paul and myself, as being the perfectionist bit and getting everything right. He was producing an album that came out quite live but is also very produced, if you know what I mean. It's got a nice edge to it and a strong sound, strong textures. And therefore, I thought he was really quite good. He and I got on extremely well and I just remember him being very supportive and encouraging. It's funny how things go. I still had certain things that didn't make it onto that album, again, that I wrote, that ended up with Gary Moore. Again, just experimenting a lot, it was an evolutionary process."

"Because like I say, when I joined UFO, I had very little input into *The Wild, the Willing* and then *Mechanix* was my first real thing, and once I start doing something, that's it, I obsess about it. That's really why I probably ended up stopping because I had done everything. I ticked all the boxes and that was it."

To reiterate, Neil therein makes an important point with respect to his involvement in the band. It is his obsession and enthusiasm that result in both *Mechanix* and even more so *Making Contact* being "Neil Carter" UFO albums—indeed the latter features nine Carter writing credits out of ten tracks.

"Yes, he had a lot more to do with that album, because of circumstances," explains Andy. "Because the band was in a bit of a state, and Neil was very together. I mean, he didn't really drink or take drugs or anything, sensible guy, and he did string arrangements, all sorts of things, wrote parts, and yes, he did get to do a bit more. Whether it's more by default than he wanted to, I don't really know. Lovely guy though, and very, very talented. I just don't think he was man enough for UFO. It was a pretty brutal band to be in, lots of practical joking, and like I say, just the drinking and drugs, especially towards the end there. It was a bit more than he could handle."

"And of course the other really sad thing was the management side of it," continues Parker. "We were so badly mismanaged, and nobody ever knew where the money went, and that was just hugely frustrating as well. Neil talks about when he left and went to Gary Moore, how everything was different, every penny was accounted for, everybody knew what was happening. With UFO, we've made fortunes and nobody knew where it went. We'd finally managed to elbow Wilf Wright out of the picture, and had in Carl Leighton-Pope, but it was a bit like shutting the stable door after the horse had bolted. We were dying a death by then, and it was just too late, really."

Asked if things ran smoother with Carl versus Wilf, Tonka says, "Not really. I'd known Carl for years and years and years. Carl had managed a local band that I was in, in 1972, so we kind of went back. It was a bit strange when Carl became our agency, because we had actually fallen out, from the local band days in Wales, years before. But around 1980, Carl was booking the band, and you would have these things in the back of your head. Anyway, you reconcile, water under the bridge, no big deal. It was only a local thing anyway, and probably the people I played with were just as fucked-up and maybe it wasn't his fault after all. So you patch things up."

"But when all that went down with Wilf, it would've been smart, really, thinking back, to get American representation. Carl kind of dived in with both feet and I don't think he was really cut out to be a manager. He was a great agent. We were always working, as you know, but it was just one of those things that I think he bit off more than he could chew, really. Pete didn't get on with him well. But when we went down—Neil and Andy and myself—to the studio outside Newbury, and started working on new material, nobody's heart was into it. But Carl used to come down there and be very supportive. Thinking about it now, from that angle, I think actually Wilf was a much better manager than Carl, when it comes to spearheading a project. Carl was, as I say, a little bit out of his depth. He's still doing the agency thing. You know he's managing the Chippendale's now—did you know that?"

Back to the Pete problem, speaking with Dmitry Epstein, Neil Carter reflected that, "I read a few things that Pete said about the direction the music was heading in, under my influence, how there were more keyboards etc., but UFO had always tried different things in the studio, long before I joined. For *Making Contact*, Paul and I had to take control and use the studio time effectively. We were a bit more organized on that one and spent several weeks writing at a hotel in Sussex before recording it at the Manor Studios in Oxfordshire."

Asked whether he could recall specific compositions that went with him to Gary Moore, Neil replies, "Yeah, 'Empty Rooms,' definitely. Because I wrote that when I was on tour with UFO. What else did I write? When UFO split up in inverted commas, Paul and Andy and I thought we might possibly do something together, but in actual fact, that was quite doomed to failure. But we did try. We went and recorded about six songs and one of those, some of it, ends up as 'Murder in the Skies' (from Moore's hit album *Victims of the Future*, issued February of '84—'Empty Rooms' is also on this record). So there was quite a lot of stuff I was writing with them in mind that ended up with Gary. Because that's when I jumped ship and went off with Gary."

"Mainly guitar," offers Carter, with respect to his main instrument for writing purposes. "When we were on tour with *Mechanix*, I took a drum box. It was the beginning of having these portable things you could take with you, like drum machines and tape recorders that you could bounce tracks off of, allowing you to actually write properly and produce a song. So I ended up on that tour we were on with Ozzy

Osbourne coming away with tons of material. Again, I had never written anything, so I was fresh. There is always stuff coming out. It might not have been entirely original, but it was my first attempt at it, really. So there was this boundless enthusiasm to get writing and do stuff."

"I like *Making Contact*, but it was recorded in a bit of an atmosphere of degeneration, because the band was coming to a bit of a halt at that point. I know they've reformed since about four times. But my incarnation of it was going down the pan, really. The parting of the way with Pete Way was mainly because we started using keyboards and we started being a bit more... I was a bit more into the American rock at that time, the emerging people that were coming out, like Heart, people that used keyboards and different techniques in the studio. We used strings, and of course, Pete wanted it to be rock 'n' roll, gritty, Rolling Stones-type rock 'n' roll. So that was the beginning of the parting of the ways with Pete, because he didn't like the music. I actually didn't realise that at the time, until afterwards. But he didn't like much of *Mechanix* at all. But there are a few quite nice songs on *Making Contact* and it was very carefully thought-out and very carefully produced and a tremendous amount of time went into it."

For his part, Andy would have liked to have been reflected more in the writing credits. "By that time, I got very frustrated with the way things had gone. In the early days we would all get together and thrash things out in a room. And if you were there and you were a part of it, you got the credit. Towards the end there, especially Paul Chapman, I would be dragged over from California, spend a month in the rehearsal room with them turning two chords into a song and get absolutely no credit whatsoever. You fight for it and somewhere between you deciding to thrash out this list of credits, and turning it into the record company, suddenly it all got changed. With the last couple of albums I got no credits whatsoever. I thought, if I'm not going to get any fucking credit, I'm not going to do any work. You tell me when the songs are written and I'll come and play on them. So the whole thing to me, it's not that I lost interest, it was more like beating your head against the wall and not getting anywhere. It was sad seeing this once great band just turning out these lacklustre performances.

"Pete left pretty much for the same reason," continues Parker. "He'd just had enough. He just rode those other things out. He didn't like all the keyboards. Pete hates keyboards. And keyboards had become quite a big part of UFO. I think Pete wanted to go back to the road more, like when we started, when we were a three-piece with a singer. That always suited him better; that was more his thing. Even today, the stuff Pete writes tends to be the more straightforward rock 'n' roll songs. So he didn't like the musical direction the band was going in, and he too was frustrated with the way things worked. Nothing against Paul, lovely guy and a good player, but I never enjoyed the band as much as I did with Michael. I think Pete feels the same. But I think his main reason would be he didn't like the way the music was going, too many keyboards. He complains even today about the keyboards."

As for where Pete was with the drug and drink, Andy says, "He was pretty out there. But in those days, he was never a problem. He always handled himself way better than the other guys. I can remember, at least for a couple years, talk of throwing up onstage every night in his performance. And Mr. Naïve, me, I didn't quite realise why he was throwing up. But Pete always handled his booze. He just had that tolerance, that constitution. So he was never really a problem and he became the front man. I think in the end, that got a bit much for him as well, having to do it all himself. Phil and Pete were very, very close for many years and then they started to drift apart.

With Pete gone, Paul and Neil split the bass duties, even breaking up guitar tasks for the record. "Paul did some bass," says Neil. "I can't remember what songs though. We sort of split it between us. In fact, when I first started off, I played bass. Subsequently I went on to play guitar. I think we used to record the backing tracks with two guitars, generally. If it was a guitar/bass song, with *Making Contact*, one of us would play guitar and one of us would play bass. On ones like 'Diesel in the Dust,' most of the rhythm guitar is me and Paul does all the lead bits. I never played lead on those albums. I actually don't think I'm a bad rhythm guitarist at all. I didn't play any guitar on any Gary Moore albums at all. I did play live, obviously. But on the records, Gary always did all the guitars."

Summing up Tonka as a guitarist, Carter calls him, "Um, good. I wouldn't say... he certainly has his moments. He's not a particularly melodic guitarist, with his solos. But he did come up with some good ideas. But I wouldn't say he's the most... you know, Schenker's solos are very melodic. But on the other hand, he used to do the same solo apparently night after night after night. Paul is much more free. He comes up with some very interesting things, which, if you sit and listen to it, there are some quite weird tonalities in what he does, actual scale-like things; he does some very odd things. But then having worked with

Gary Moore subsequently, you know, there's no comparison for me. Personally, I've only met Michael really through Wild Horses. That's the only time I ever had any contact with Michael. He used to come along to gigs when I played with Wild Horses. He's a troubled man, isn't he?"

"He can drink anyone under the table," adds Neil, back on the subject of Tonka, his co-guitarist, specifically the man's constitution. "He's the sort of person that when he drinks, he goes into complete overdrive. It's just the way he is. He's a big person, big personality, and he still is. I spoke to him a few years ago and he hasn't changed a bit. But he's a good-hearted person, a very, very good-hearted person, very warm. No edge to him whatsoever. He just enjoyed the party, I think. Most people like that, they just enjoy the party."

"From my point of view, I'm a little person who doesn't actually... you know, I have no capacity for drink or anything. I wouldn't do it because I just can't do it. Whereas a man like that has got a big constitution and can drink copious amounts. I work with people now who for some reason drink copious amounts and still function. But occasionally he had to take control because the tour manager would be so out of it and everyone else would be so out of it. But I wouldn't put myself in that category (laughs). Dear oh dear. But he's a very nice guy, and he's almost like a relative. You wouldn't see him for twenty years, and then all of a sudden you meet him and it's like the day you last saw him. Nice to speak to you."

But back in 1982, the party was still raging hard, and UFO, against all odds, were trying to finish up important business before the year was out. "*Making Contact* was difficult and I think that was when Pete disappeared," says an ever-wry Phil Mogg, summing up the experience with characteristic opacity. "He said he was coming to the rehearsals and I spoke to him and he said, 'Oh, yeah, yeah, I'll be there next week' and the next thing I read he'd gone off with Eddie Clarke to form Fastway. So he obviously wasn't coming down to rehearsals. So that was a bit of a difficult album. We rehearsed in Hastings, down by the sea. I'm a bit vague on that. That was our vague period."

In any event, there was indeed a record fashioned out of chaos, *Making Contact*, released in February '83, exactly a year after its predecessor, opening in dramatic fashion with "Blinded by a Lie," featuring a Carter keyboard wash giving way to a solid, even stern metal riff, buttressed by more keys, fading to a stark verse featuring Phil over even more keyboards. Despite all this polish, the track is a heads-down rocker, gruff of purpose, laconic of melody.

Chapman intimates that Phil's "Blinded by a Lie" lyric was written in dedication to the band's ex-manager Wilf Wright. "Wilf did a lot of things without us knowing, like cross-collateralizing certain things, where publishing money would end up going to pay a record bill. In actual fact I was reading that book with Rory Gallagher, Steve Marriott and Robin Trower (ed. *Gallagher Marriott Derringer & Trower*, by Dan Muise, Hal Leonard Corporation). I knew some of those guys, because when I was in an Irish band, Skid Row, Rory and I, we used to play together and we would frequently see each other. And then Steve Marriott and Jerry Shirley... Jerry was in Waysted."

"Robin Trower is one of the most interesting ones, because I never actually met Robin Trower. But Wilf managed Robin Trower the same time he was managing UFO. Or he was just finishing managing Robin, because he was also on Chrysalis. When I first went to L.A. with my wife, I was staying with Wilf, in his house. I was looking for something, and I looked under his stairs and I opened it, and there are all these masters in there, two-inch tapes, racks of them, of *Bridge of Sighs* and all of Robin's records, all under the stairs. And I'm going, holy shit!"

"Jimmy Dewar, the bass player had come around; he'd just discovered Jesus. There are some interesting articles in that book. Derek Sutton, who used to manage Styx and a few other people, he was friendly with Wilf, but Derek Sutton had some interesting observations of Wilf's managing of Robin Trower in that book. He said Wilf didn't intentionally try to rip people off. I don't think Wilf was actually dishonest. He just didn't know what to do. He just made bad decisions because he thought that was the right decision. It wasn't an intentional thing. I beg to differ a bit on that. Some of that is true. He got involved with The Cult after UFO, and all of a sudden, The Cult just ceased to exist (laughs). You know what I mean? Everything Wilf got involved with, something kind of happened. You could never put your finger on it. He's working for Jimmy Page now. He's living in Fort Lauderdale."

"But there were some decisions made there. To be honest, I was fresh in the band. Wilf used to play these stupid fucking mind games with everybody. I mean, I'd seen Wilf... When we played in Germany one time, we did a TV show in Dortmund and I actually have it on DVD; it's really good. Even now it still kind of holds up. But he'd pulled over for the day, to pick up the money or see how it was going or whatever, from London, spend the night, and fly back the next morning."

"UFO's tour manager had driven the band right from northern Italy or something like that. The guy's fried; he'd been working his tail off for months. Wilf is at a different hotel and I'm in this hotel with John and we were at the bar. We had just gotten back from the show. The phone goes, 'Mr. Knowles, Mr. Knowles.' It's Wilf on the phone, in the other hotel 15, 20 kilometers away, ordering John to get up—because he thought he might been in bed; he didn't care—ordering John to get up, get dressed, go and get the car in the car park, and drive to a club that he had located in downtown Dortmund and buy him a bottle of Canadian Club and mixers, and deliver it to his hotel. John did it. I said, 'You must be out of your friggin' mind.' He actually went and did it. That's the kind of stuff that Wilf would do to people."

"I can remember... listen to this one. He got involved with Waysted. I said to Pete, 'If he's involved, I'm walking.' Which is basically kind of what happened the first time, in a roundabout way. I can remember, I was sending part of my per diems home, because my wife had just had another baby. We had four kids under the age of ten, right? I'm on the road and she's getting ready to move back to America and I said, 'Listen, I'll send you some cash.' I'm sending half of my per diems home, which, I shouldn't really have to do. Wilf should have taken care of it. You know, the money was always late. 'Oh, it was transferred' da da da da. 'No it wasn't transferred.'"

"Wilf would fuckin' bullshit. This guy had come over, who used to work for Morris Johns who did the Knebworth shows, this guy called Dee, assistant tour manager. I said, 'What the hell is he doing here?! We don't need an assistant tour manager!' He's giving Dee money to go and get hookers! I mean, I'm next door to him in the Toronto Hilton or whatever the hell we were at in Toronto, and there's all these women going next door. There's a big party going on. I didn't drink for nine months in that whole thing. I'm lying there reading a book going, 'What the fuck is going... what a messed-up fucking zoo this is.' You know, they're all in there drunk and partying and doing lines of coke with hookers and everything, and I'm in the band, in the other room with no money reading a book. I'm looking at this whole thing and going, 'What's wrong with this picture?' That's a Wilfism right there. He'd come over and stay in a different hotel, which would always be a five-star hotel. There'd always be shady goings-on there and then he'd leave. That kind of thing. It was a shame, really."

"But no, *Making Contact*, everybody was in a bit of a haze, from outside substances. It was sad, because if everything would've been done correctly, if maybe we would've gotten out of the Carl situation and into a different management, and maybe found a bass player that was a permanent bass player that took Pete's place, and we actually straightened up just a little bit, the band probably could've gone on for a long, long time."

"I think 'Blinded by a Lie' ended up really well," says Neil back on *Making Contact*'s apparently Wilf-inspired opening track. "Actually, it's quite interesting, because I get royalties for performance and things; it comes through and the ones that get played are 'Blinded by a Lie' and 'Call My Name,' as well as 'The Way the Wild Wind Blows'—they still play those. Goodness knows where, probably like Hungary and Romania. But when I get my royalty statements, it's always quite interesting to read where they actually do play these things. I can't say I actually get any royalties for actual sales. Typical UFO. Nobody actually makes a penny from it. But anyway..."

After "Blinded by a Lie" came a tale of duplicitous paperwork, the murky dealings kept coming, "Diesel in the Dust" painting a film noire picture of murder and the silence of a community quietly glad that it had occurred. Says Tonka, "Phil took that from a story in Rolling Stone; it's a true story, about how they covered up the murder. Even the character is named by name—Ted McKinley; that was the guy."

Confirms Andy, "Phil wrote that because it was a true story about some town that had this bully guy that was ruining everyone's life in this town, and the whole town ganged up and got rid of him (laughs). I think Phil got it out of the newspaper over here. But they knew, and I think maybe even the local sheriff was turning a blind eye, because this guy was such a pain in the ass."

Once again, Phil marries a great story—or at least the seductive fragments of one—to a snarling musical track, the "Diesel" riff being both malevolent and a bit complicated, the track being a favourite of Neil Carter's, along with "When It's Time to Rock." Characteristically (and character-building?) for UFO, the song breaks bright for a melodic chorus, giving the track in the aggregate a sense of light and dark hues, resulting in another triumphant composition despite the crushing adversity inflicted (and self-inflicted) on the band at the time.

"Whoa, I love both of those," remarks Tonka on the record's opening one-two punch. "Actually they were basically Neil's. Well, it says on the thing. I always ended up putting the middles in, the little Eddie Van Halen bits in the middle, the solos, which really weren't creditable because they weren't really part of the song."

Next up was a gorgeous pop metal rocker called "A Fool for Love" (not to be confused with *No Heavy Petting*'s "A Fool in Love!"), which just might house UFO's hookiest chorus ever. Phil turns in a nice, sympathetic lyric about the miles-apart motivations between men and women. As well, he seals the song's success with a few characteristically Moggy "la la las".

"Actually, that's quite good," recalls Carter. "It's got a lot of keyboards and that's actually my obsession with Journey again. That's quite a nice song, that. But again, I have to admit, I did have quite a lot to do with that album. Rightly or wrongly, there wasn't much else coming in. It was Paul and me and Phil, really, at that point. Andy never really wrote anything so it was down to myself, Paul and Phil to actually do it. But I was vaguely proud of that album. Certain things I would possibly change, but it was something that was really done in adversity. We started off with Gary Lyons; it wasn't working, and we got someone else in. It turned out quite well, and it was actually my first chance of really taking control of something and having a big input into it. Whether I would class it as a classic UFO album, I don't know. To me, the classic ones are the ones I'm not on. But even still, I'm quite proud of it."

"Keyboard-wise, I was experimenting with synthesizers and stuff," adds Carter. "You have to remember, this was at the start of things like the Oberheim and the other thing I had, the Prophet 5—all of those polyphonic keyboards had just become common things. I don't take much credit for many things, but I was actually one of the first rock keyboard players to use polyphonic synthesizers and sequencers but also sampling keyboards as well. Anything new, I was fascinated by. I wanted to get hold of it and use it. There were lots of other keyboard players using them, but I do count myself as one of the ones that started using them quite early on."

"So yes, there are some good keyboard bits on *Making Contact*. It's not particularly flashy keyboards, but it's nice sounds, good strings and good effects. It's not real strings, but rather all keyboard stuff. No strings at all. But there were some very good strings sounds on the Prophet 5 that we used, and before that, we used on *Mechanix* Mellotrons and stuff like that. On 'Somethin' Else,' we used Mellotrons. It's interesting to experiment with these things. Referring to what I said about Pete, perhaps it doesn't really define UFO, keyboards. But you have to move with the times. You can't just stand still. You have to try things, and if they work, whatever. But in hindsight, I think some of the best stuff is 'Lights Out' and 'Too Hot to Handle.' These are the classic UFO songs. I don't actually feel that anything I did with them was particularly classic UFO, to be honest and that comes from the heart. I like what we did, but

I think their classic tracks are those older ones that everyone loves."

"You and Me" follows, UFO offering a lush and fully committed ballad filled to the brim with the keyboard sounds synonymous with the '80s that Neil talks about, Tonka adding an atmospheric guitar solo for good measure. The track is reminiscent of Led Zeppelin's "All My Love," mirroring that classic's angelic, surging yet light keyboard pulse, Phil penning a lyric about a man and woman forced, for the time being, to eke out an existence on their love alone.

"'You and Me,' I played a fretless bass on that," notes Paul. "In actual fact, I have a demo of that somewhere on tape, a working tape of Phil's. I don't know how I ended up with it. I put it on looking for something else on it years ago, and Phil is singing on it, over a keyboard. I think he was trying to play keyboards on it, and it was Neil's idea and it's so flat! I put it on and I would be like, 'Oh man, if ever I wanted to blackmail somebody' (laughs). It wasn't his fault. But yes, I have a magnificent, incredibly flat version of 'You and Me,' just like one verse. I remember that Carl Leighton-Pope was managing the band at the time and he was in the studio and I wasn't there. He told them to turn the solo down at the end and put all the echo on it. I came in, and it was already being mixed, and I was like, 'What the hell is that?' He said, 'Well, I thought...' 'Fuckin' 'ell, you stick to managing and let me stick to playing guitar.' So, it turned into a bit of a muddy solo at the end."

Closing side one of the original vinyl is "When It's Time to Rock," a fastback rocker that opens grandly very much like Rush's "The Spirit of Radio." Credited to Chapman/Mogg, it is the only non-Carter tune on the album and it's a ripper, once more the band rising to the hard rock challenge with a fairly advanced central riff, with Phil matching the ambition of the musical track with a lyric that mixes up wonderfully images of gang violence with world-beating rock 'n' roll heroics. "When It's Time to Rock" was the album's only single, issued three months after *Making Contact*'s launch, with the non-LP "Everybody Knows"—a bracing, classy, snarling hard rocker credited to Chapman/Mogg—as its b-side. It rose to an unimpressive No.70 in the UK charts. The 12" version of the single added "Push It's Love" for potent measure, resulting in a very heavy three-tracker indeed.

"When It's Time to Rock" is a production tour de force, indeed representative of this idea that the album was over-worked, over-produced, to the point of a palpable soulnessness.

"The idea behind that song was that it was going to be like another 'Rock Bottom,'" reflects Chapman. "The riff and the length of the song and the feel of the whole thing, the idea behind it… but you have to remember, it was right at the end of the band. You know, everything is technically in the right place, but I agree, it just doesn't have the feel of the older stuff. But I really like the album and Mick Glossop was great. Bearing in mind he had to come in and clean up a huge mess, which is basically what it was from a musical standpoint. It was just a big cluster, including who was going to play what on what tracks. Neil wanted to play bass on things, I wanted to play bass on things. Mick really did a good job of coming in and putting it all together."

Then there were the multiple studios used, officially according to the credits, a total of four. "Yes, everything was running late and we ended up moving from studio to studio," continues Chapman. "Everything was supposed to be done, initially, at The Manor. The only thing was, with a late beginning, it was well over a week into the whole thing, actually first with Gary Lyons. Obviously we didn't finish, and The Town House was the next one; that was the other Richard Branson thing in Shepherds Bush around central London and of course, we were trying to find time anywhere we could. Carl was phoning around, or maybe it was Roy Ellis, but somebody was trying to book us time in whatever place we could find."

"The Maison Rouge thing was Ian Anderson's studio. That was the last one, in Fulham Road; I can remember that, right before the end of the last mixes. That's why we ended up in all those places. It actually helped, because every time you go from one room to another, you re-calibrate everything. It all sounds different, and you go, oh, is that what we did there? When did we put that down? By the time you get to Maison Rouge, you're thinking, oh, this sounds much better than that room, let's redo it (laughs) and you'd end up running out even over more time."

Asked if Ian Anderson ever showed up to look in on the guys, Chapman says, "No. The only thing I can remember about working at Maison Rouge, was that *Poltergeist* movie had just come out. They had a video shop next door, close to the studio, just down the street. They had a deal with the video guy, where you get bootleg videos. He could come and watch the bands record and things like that, and I can remember walking out of there with a bootleg copy of *E.T.* and *Poltergeist*, before they were out on video. I can remember Men at Work; somebody was playing 'Who Can It Be Now?' That's all I remember. And they had a bar in the studio as well. Maybe that's why I can't remember it too well (laughs)."

I asked Chapman if watching these movies inspired the title of the record, *Making Contact*. "No, that was hanging around a while," says Tonka. "In fact, I believe, when I rejoined the band in 1978, we were in Los Angeles, and there were names being thrown around for the double live album, and there was a short list. I was staying with Wilf in the main band house, where the office was in Los Angeles, and I think everybody put in two or three ideas on a piece of paper, for *Strangers in the Night*. One of the ones I put in was *Out of the Darkness* and then *Making Contact* and something else. So it had been floating around for a while."

The cover art chosen for the record, as oblique as it is, represents the title smartly—it's a naked woman telephone operator, two arms in motion to look like six, making connections, electronically albeit old school. "I remember that because my girlfriend had gone back to Florida the day after New Year's Day," recalls Chapman. "And it was that week I was at Chrysalis, looking at various different suggestions and ideas, and we ended up going with that one, and I don't remember why. But I don't think it was Hipgnosis, although Storm Thorgerson did the photography. The woman with the bum. He was always into being weird via body parts. But yes, I can remember being at Chrysalis with Neil and Carl Leighton-Pope, okaying art."

Back to "When It's Time to Rock" and its somewhat over-baked production, Paul is in total agreement that things got over-analysed.

"Yes, they were, and if you consider the circumstances that it was created under, you have to realise that we actually pulled it off to a point. You have to bear in mind that the summer before, when we were doing the *Mechanix* thing, that was the tour with Ozzy and the bat's head and Randy Rhoads. We were out probably until August or something like that, from January. Then things would come up where we would do the odd festival, or we would come home to do some writing. That's when all hell broke loose at my house."

"Then we did the European tour and one thing or another, and before you look around, you fly back after having an absolutely blinding year. When I came back to my apartment in Florida, Christmas of '82, '83, like I say, going over with Neil to Chrysalis, it was the first time I had been home in about three months, right? When I went back to Britain... because I lived in Florida, my girlfriend flew back the day after New Year's Day, and I got home June 6th. I was gone a whole another six months! That's how it was."

"I have a thing now, if you don't come with me, I'm never going to be away for more than three weeks. You get to a certain point where you go what's the point? I mean, to go for six months and do that whole thing, everybody was frazzled. Everybody! You're talking about really fucking fried here. To pull an album out in the middle of all that, it was really a tall order, when you think about it. I think we did pretty good under the circumstances."

"Considering the whole Gary balls-up and everything. When we got out, I think we started playing in Poland January 5th or something like that. At the beginning of all that, she left on the 2nd, and I went back to London from Wales, and I think the day after that, Billy Sheehan arrived. Then I got a day of breaking Billy into the band in a hotel room, and then two or three days of rehearsal, and then right to Poland and the whole thing just starts all over again, including playing all the new stuff, which we had only really just finished. There wasn't any breathing space, is what I'm trying to tell you. I can remember a bit of trivia. I remember rehearsing at John Henry's, before going to Poland, and I can remember Phil Collen had come down and gave me and unmixed copy of where they were so far with *Pyromania* and I gave him a copy of *Making Contact*. Because it wasn't out yet; it was still being pressed or whatever."

Side two of *Making Contact*—more on Poland and Billy Sheehan later!—opens with "The Way the Wild Wind Blows," another energetic rocker built around a combative riff and quite pleasingly, a melodic, eminently singable chorus, with Phil placing himself at the centre of a getaway chase straight to the county jail.

"That was another Lone Star one," offers Paul. "I have a tape of the jam of that with nearly the whole thing, but not as organized as how it ended up there. The funny thing about that album, was that I was going through a divorce at the time, when we were writing that. That was probably my least input album of all the albums we did. I came back and I'm supposed to be writing for the album and all hell is breaking loose in my house. Plus we were coming off the road and going right in. Neil had been working and he had tons and tons of stuff. He had more on that album than on any other and I probably had the least."

"Like I say, "The Way the Wild Wind Blows" was a hangover from a Lone Star thing that I had a long, long time before, as were a lot of other songs, like "No Place to Run," "Long Gone"—"This Fire Burns Tonight" is "Travelling Man." "The Way the Wild Wind Blows" is one of my favourite tracks on the album from a playing point of view. I really enjoyed playing it. I love the bass playing on the end of it; I was pretty proud of that. Actually, I'm playing with Andy on that. Because everything is done separately now. When you layer records, it's not as creative as it used to be. Everything is ProTools, you edit things out, trim here, truncate that, do this. Whereas back then, you were playing in the same room at the same time. 'Ah we'll add the bass later.' 'No, let's do it now.' That type of thing and we played pretty well on that."

"Yes, we used to always put the drums and bass on together," affirms Andy. "And quite often, it would be all four of us in there, other than Phil. We never knew what Phil was going to do. There was only one album in my entire career with these guys, where I knew what the vocals were going to be, and that was *Walk on Water*. He actually had quite well prepared vocals for that. But we had no idea what he was going to do on *Making Contact*. We only had working titles, just names picked out of the blue, because there were no lyrics—you didn't have a title, nothing to call it. You could just call them tracks 1, 2, and 3, but we put funny, weird titles on them anyway."

"Call My Name" is next, the narrator telling the apocryphal tale of a working girl rescued from the street corners of the night through love. Musically, this one's a little treacly—no wonder, given Neil Carter's explanation of its development. "'Call My Name,' almost completely written by me, but with Phil's lyrics. I was influenced by Bryan Adams at that point. I used to think he was wonderful. I remember, we did a festival, an MTV thing, I think, in Florida, and Bryan Adams was the opening act, on one of his first tours, and his album was starting to break really big. I quite liked him and that song was going along those lines. I remember thinking I'd like to write something like that."

It's back to the rock for "All Over You," which contains a similar antagonistic vibe to "Diesel in the Dust," Phil powerful on vocals, the track pounding along to a strong rhythm bed and not much of a riff. The lyric is a standard woman done me wrong, although the queen of Texas reference might lean it a bit autobiographical towards Phil's stormy relationship with "the famous Jean."

"'No Getaway' might have been a thrown-together type song," chips in Carter, with respect to the album's second to last track, a standard, basic, meat and potatoes rocker about the classic stalker relationship—obsessed male fan and female film star. "No Getaway" marks a rare instance where things actually go south with a UFO chorus, this track humming along acceptably and then souring with an anticlimactic, sort of sadly melodic chorus break.

But the record closes strongly, "Push, It's Love" being a rhythmic and roaring heavy metal workout, kicked off by rambunctious drums, Tonka joining in with a memorable bass lick. "I get bootlegs given to me and I think Andy was excellent," says Paul, on UFO's unsung drummer. "He's very innovative. In a way, I would say he's better than Jason (Bonham—UFO's sticksman at the time of this chat). He was innovative, because Andy was following Jason's father. And Jason, to a certain extent, as good as I think he is, he's a copier as opposed to being an innovator, you know what I mean? It's only that I say that compared to Andy because Andy got very good. I listen to stuff from the bootlegs and I go, 'Well, that's really good.' I hear what it was about the band that many people go, 'Ooh, that's good.' Chemistry's the word. That's what music is all about."

With *Making Contact* in the can and the band hitting the road, one of many memorable tour debacles of this record's tour cycle actually occurs before the record is put in the shops.

"We made that album in 1982, and the band had completely folded by April of '83—that was it," explains Andy, offering a bit of context before relating what happened in Poland and Greece. "We all left and Phil just went into rehab or whatever he did, and then just carried on for the sake of the band. But things were pretty much in tatters by then. I was living in California still. My daughter would've been two, going on three, and for me at that time, I was still doing it because it's basically all I knew how to do. But the band was in a real state. The substance abuse was out of control by then, with Paul and Phil, plus Pete was gone. Paul and Neil did the bass on the album between them. We didn't even have a bass player to do that one."

"But we went to Poland first, and our bass player for that was Billy Sheehan," continues Andy. "That was not bad. Then we did Spain and Italy, and when we got to Athens, Greece, that's where it all fell apart. Billy was having to go back. Athens was going to be his last show. Paul Gray was ready to take over. I remember we went on stage at this place in Athens and it held about 2000 or 3000 people and they were just screaming. They wanted the band quite badly. I remember it was quite cold there and I was surprised. But the place was packed and they were screaming for the band."

"But because we were late getting on there, they were screaming *at* us rather than *for* us, and they were lobbing cans of beer up on the stage. Billy Sheehan got hit. He's such a huge guy, nice big target, and he got hit in the forehead with a full can of beer. He had a bruise like a boiled egg sticking out of his forehead, like a lump on his head. I remember looking out and the whole thing was a shambles and such a mess. I remember looking over and seeing Paul Gray standing in the wings with this look of absolute fear, that he was going to have to take over the next day and do this."

"Even back in Poland, I broke up a huge fight between Tonka and Phil. It was getting to the point where it was over. It was just going through the motions. We were doing "Lights Out," and it was time for the vocals to come back in, and there were no vocals. We're thinking, where the fuck is he? We couldn't see him. There was no vocals, and I felt something behind me, and he was on the back of the riser and he was completely broken down. Phil was virtually in tears. He couldn't sing. He was just gone, and he had overdone it, and that was it."

"We struggled through the rest of the show with him, came offstage, and he's standing in the dressing room. It's quite cold in there and they had one of those little old-fashioned heaters with the glowing gold bars in it. He was standing with his back to it; it's down on the floor. The next thing I know, he had fallen back, had just passed-out falling back and he was laying over this damn thing, you know, with his legs there. I just quickly picked him up, slung him over my shoulder and took him out and put him on the bus, and thought, this is that, we cannot do this anymore. We're doing more harm than good here. This guy needs to go home, he just needs to go to a hospital or something. He's fucked-up."

"So we cancelled the rest of the tour, which was pretty bad. That would've been it, but our friend Adrian Hopkins, for the English tour, had already laid out all the money, and the English tour was starting in March. So we thought Phil would take a couple or three weeks between this run and the English run and straighten himself up, and we would at least do this English tour so Adrian wouldn't lose his shirt."

"Which we did, but even that was heartbreaking. By that time it was hard to be around it. Even the albums, I would come in, do the album and fly out. For obvious reasons—Tonka and Phil were heavily into smack at that time. Poor Neil Carter; he was the straightest one in the band. Which was really hard for him. I remember that fight in Poland, Tonka and Phil are knocking six bells out of each other after the show. Tonka had no shirt on, and Phil had him pinned against this old-fashioned cast-iron radiator. The thing was blistering, man. It was burning his back and he was screaming, so I dragged him off, and I was in the middle of them trying to hold them apart. I look around, and poor little Neil was cowering under the table in the dressing room. It was just brutal."

Oddly, the band's Polish excursion was sponsored by amplifier company Vox. "Yes, we were using some Vox gear. I don't think it wasn't per se that it was bad, but it just didn't take to travelling. Every time we got to the gig, bits just dropped off of it and it wasn't working and things had come loose inside or it was just going adrift. We had a lot of trouble that year, absolutely. We were hurting. We were trying to take whatever we could get, and I think Vox offered us all this gear and we thought it was a good idea, but it didn't hold up to the travel on the road. Marshalls had been kicked over and stomped on and those things are bulletproof and still are. But the Vox gear really suffered, especially in Poland where some of the roads were really terrible. So they didn't like being shipped around, and we had a lot of trouble with them at the shows, and the guys were tearing them apart trying to get them to work."

As Andy mentioned, the band knocked it on the head, never finished the tour. "There were still a lot of that tour to go. We were supposed to go to Yugoslavia, Germany, Scandinavia, and we just cancelled it. There was no point. I had no communication with Phil at that time. We had grown apart because he was so fucked-up. I was just so angry and bitter about the whole thing, I'd spent my whole life doing this and it's all going to nothing. There's no way I could even talk to him back then, so it was like a decision, this is it, we've got to stop this or somebody's going to end up dead."

"So we did, and the last thing we did was the English tour. I don't know what happened to the gear from Athens. The gear must've made it back because we obviously did the English tour. There may have been a problem with the promoter. It's a bit fuzzy for me. Because of my state of mind, I don't remember some of that stuff—I've blocked it out. I was just very miserable. You tried as hard as you could, and if you're soundman sucked, your band sucked. It was really struggling back then. I know he mentioned himself that it was a dark time for UFO."

Incoming bassist Paul Gray, in conversation with UFO den mother Kate Battttttty (sic) from beloved UFO fan site Strangers in the Night, had this to say about the 1983 disintegration of the band: "After a few days travelling around Spain and France in the cars with them, I realised that if they continued at the pace they were at, something was gonna give sooner or later. Let's say the party started when we were turfed out of bed by tour manager John Knowles, and sometimes that was 7AM. So not surprised, but disappointed, yeah. I'd left The Damned to do a world tour with UFO and managed one bleedin' gig in a windswept Greek stadium!"

"The '83 tour was pretty daunting for me, learning a whole bunch of unfamiliar songs very quickly. We never actually rehearsed all together as far as I can recall, although we did all manage to meet in the pub next to Nomis Studios. By the time I felt comfortable onstage enough to relax, the bloody thing was over! Also it was then that I realised the shadow of Mr. Way loomed large. Plus everyone knew it was the end so it wasn't the most 'up' of tours. But I loved playing with the band—great gigs, perfect sound, good company, and excellent crew. The '85-'88 line-up was more comfortable as it was a 'new start' for the band. I know Phil was hesitant about calling it UFO for a while. But I got on really well with Phil and we spent a lot of time knocking song ideas around together, and I had quite a lot of input into the band. The tours were great, especially in the US, and I can't remember not actually enjoying every minute of it. I'd have loved it to have continued."

Phil reaches way back to chart the slippery slope toward the band's first break-up. "Well Michael left, then came back to do the *Strangers in the Night* tour and album and went completely after that. We were left with that album, which was our biggest chart success in England, and without a guitarist. I think his departure was a little bit rash because we had so much work coming in. We had played with Paul Chapman before, so we got him in because he knew most of the material. We practiced for six days and played the Chicago Amphitheater for two nights. We did it, but we'd never do a thing like that now because it takes time to find some sort of replacement who will be either different or at least come up to par with Schenker's talents in terms of writing and playing. You can't rush those things and I think we did. We managed to get on under those situations—Paul Raymond went; Neil Carter came in—but I think everything was gradually getting worn down and we weren't seeing much success. As a matter of fact, everything was going downhill. It got to a point where everything was fucked. You couldn't see any light at the end of the tunnel, or any reason why you were still doing it, so we packed it all in, in 1983."

"It's funny, because I gave a talk about that," says Neil—to reiterate, at this point, a music teacher in Brighton—with respect to the Greek debacle. "I'm a house tutor in the school I'm at, a house master. I gave this talk to the boys, because it's all gone very retro in England. All these kids love all these bands and they're all aware of my past, and it's fantastic for them, because they've got a real live, sort of relic from the

'80s. So I was actually telling them about Greece and having to stand behind the amps while we were being bottled by these Greek people who paid all this money to see us. We were playing one song, and Phil was still singing the one before. So it was rather awful, just chronic. It really was, that whole tour, absolutely chronic. Just watching something disintegrate in front of your eyes."

"We had Billy Sheehan on bass, who was very professional. He wasn't a good bassist for UFO but he was very professional. It's people living out their... it's just whether things work. UFO didn't need a Billy Sheehan-type bassist; put it that way. It wasn't that sort of band. You know, Billy has great talents but it just wasn't his band, and I think he knew that. But it was nice having someone who was very enthusiastic, professional. I think he was appalled, to be honest, by the behaviour of some of the group. Yeah, utterly appalled. Then we had Paul Gray come in for the last night. Paul was going to do the rest of the tour, but we just said, 'We're going home.' We didn't want to do it. All of us decided, independently of Phil, that we had just had enough and we wanted to go home. So we cancelled the rest of the tour. But we did the final tour of England. The European tour was utterly vile, it really was, a thing to be got through. We had just had enough and said that's it."

"We were seven or eight songs in," says Neil, elaborating, on the final straw. "I just remember it being appalling and then obviously the kids just really twigged that there was something seriously not right, and they started throwing bottles. But it's funny how memory erases certain things. I don't remember much about that tour, except listening to the new Journey album constantly and then that show, and then I think Phil throwing a mirror out the window—that was quite charming. But the band, if you look at the history of the group, there's always these things going on, even well after I stopped playing, with dreadful things happening with Michael Schenker."

As for Phil's main problem at this point of implosion, "It was just perhaps travelling too long in the role," muses Carter. "I don't know, to be honest. I think it was just boredom, perhaps having done it too many times. It's usually alcohol-related or something. I wouldn't like to swear by it. They're all great drinkers and whatevers, and a lot of stuff has been said over the years about the excesses of the group and I don't need to add to it. It's just typical of UFO, a UFOism, always an accident waiting to happen. Great moments, but some bloody awful ones as well."

"Yes, many disasters," chuckles Billy Sheehan, recalling his whirlwind tour with the boys, correcting the leading question that the Greek tragedy was the main or only "disaster."

"Actually when I got home from the UFO tour, Spinal Tap came out and I went to see it and it wasn't funny; it wasn't funny at all (laughs). I just lived it. But I love those guys; they're wonderful people. They were just caught in a horrible situation, their lives, their career… it happens. I toured with them in 1983. Pete Way had left the band and we had all these—at the time—oddball markets in Europe. Instead of England and Germany, we did Poland, Greece, Spain, Portugal, some unusual places. The band was under high pressure because they were a little bit splintered up to start with. I give them that. You have to cut them some slack because they were under a lot of pressure."

"But in Greece, we got there and the promoter gave all of us a huge bottle of Metaxa brandy with a spigot at the bottom of it. It was too big to pour. You had to have a faucet at the bottom. We were in the hotel, and I went up to the roof of the hotel and I was looking out at the Parthenon, all this Greek architecture, and I go back down to the hotel and I walk by Phil's room and the bottle is outside in front of his door empty. I'm thinking, oh no, we're doomed! So Phil had been drinking a little bit and we got up onstage and he couldn't function; he could barely stand up. So I ended up singing parts of 'Lights Out,' 'Rock Bottom' and stuff. Phil comes back to me and I'm standing by my amp because people are throwing so much shit at him because he's just too fucked-up to play and they're pissed off."

"So I'm back by my amp so I don't get hit. So he rolls back to me and in the worst English barely discernible drunken drawl, 'Billy, I think if you come to the front of the stage, we can get them, we can win them over.' So I walked out to the front of the stage and somebody had just thrown a huge firecracker before that, and pushed Phil even further into submission and something hit me in the head. I thought a firecracker blew off in my face, because it was just like getting punched in the face and I didn't know what happened. And someone had wadded up some kind of a tin can and thrown it from about a hundred yards back and it hit me in the head. I went to the side of the stage, still playing—I didn't stop playing—and the crew guys are all standing there with flashlights and I yelled out, 'Is it bleeding?!' And they're looking at each other and they go, 'Should we tell him?!' (laughs). So obviously blood was pouring out of my head and I went back and gave the crowd the finger and showed them my ass and pointed to it as if they could kiss it; I was pretty pissed-off. But the show ended, and we got done, and I got out of there okay."

The story goes that the band all jumped on a plane and just flew out of there, leaving everything behind. True? "Yes, the next morning; but I didn't hear that story of them leaving everything behind. They had an endorsement deal with Vox. Vox gave them all these amps. Paul Chapman had about twenty amps set up onstage and by the fourth gig in Poland there was only one left working. Then eventually he had to plug in direct to the board because all the amps had fried. And that was the first country of the tour, so we had a lot of equipment problems on that tour."

"But it was an amazing experience. Playing with UFO first of all, was great, interesting—they're a legendary band. When I got to England in '83 for rehearsals, I had been sleep-learning all the tracks at the Talas shows, with the cassette thing on. They gave me a list of about thirty songs they wanted to play, and I really knew them well. I listened to them over and over and over again, so when I got to England I thought, we'll have to rehearse all the songs."

"So the first rehearsal, I get there about noon, the other guys show up about 4:00, talk for a little while, took a break around 5:30, go to the pub, got back half in the bag about 8:00, decided to knock it off about 10:00—and we still hadn't run through one song. The next day, the same thing happens. By the third day I said, 'You know, guys, can we go through this shit?' But we had a couple of good shows. Paul Chapman is a great player, Andy Parker was really good, the keyboard player/singer... I forgot his name, he played with Gary Moore later on. I like Phil a lot, and I even like Michael. He's a sweet guy and the music business is a tough grind, so you put the two together and you're going to have trouble, you know? I think if Michael wouldn't have gone down some of the wrong roads, you know... he's a great player, kind of shy and reserved, but when he goes onstage it's amazing. I've seen Michael play on some of the early UFO show's I'd seen and he's spectacular. Talas opened up for UFO a couple times; that's what made the connection."

"I had worked with Michael Schenker in '79 on his solo record," continues Billy, adding to the pile of people that might have become part of MSG. "Myself and Denny Carmassi... we didn't end up recording the record because Michael went off the deep end. They called us to come back and neither of us wanted to do it. This was his very first solo album, but I wasn't involved. I found a bootleg of it in Japan that was all the demos that I played on. There's actually a photo of Michael sitting in a chair with all this tape stuck to him and it says Michael Schenker with Billy Sheehan. So I got that—I should put it on my website. It was recordings of most of the songs. I had rehearsed all the songs, but then Michael kind went off the deep end, cut off his hair, smashed his Flying V. Me and Denny Carmassi went over to his apartment and fixed it up so he wouldn't get charged; we picked up the pieces of his guitar with his wife or girlfriend Gabriella, then we went home and they called us a few months later to come back and we said, 'You know? We're kind of busy right now.'"

Finally, Paul Chapman's recollection of the debacle goes this way: "The very first gig we did was in Poland, January of '83, and I had all brand new equipment—not the best place in the world to start a tour, not then anyway. I was using Vox gear instead of Marshall, because I was endorsing Vox and I had the Vox factory at my beck and call, and everything blew up. In Poland it's hard enough finding food, let alone tubes for Vox amps; it's a tricky situation. It was Billy's first gig and we walked off the stage and Phil and I got into a major fistfight. I mean, you're talking brutal, like broken shoulders and blood and all kinds of shit. Billy was like, 'What the hell have I stepped into?!' That's when the band broke up, on that European tour."

On assimilating Billy Sheehan's actual style of playing—the note-dense polar opposite of Pete's—Tonka indeed intimates that, that was a problem. "Well, that was a bone of contention between him and Andy," says Paul. "He had to kind of cut corners a lot. We said look, have a bass solo for as long as you want and put all the notes in that part. Take them out everywhere else and put them in that part. But when he did the David Lee Roth thing, it was more in that direction, 'You play it like this or don't be here.' If you listen to 'Yankee Rose,' he was just peddling straight eights. If that had been Talas, it wouldn't have sounded like that (laughs)."

Asked whether they were successful in reining Billy in Chapman says, "We tried to. You get that impending feeling of doom—the situation the band was in at the time. At that point, all I could think of was coming home. To be honest, the actual thought of going out for another five months, seven months, forget it. Whereas if someone asked me right now, I would be like, 'Oh, lovely!' But at the time, you know, the grass is always greener, or in my case, the beach was always whiter. I just wanted to go home and lie on the beach and have a rest. It got to the point where I hadn't seen my kids, my wife... well, I had just gone through a divorce. My first wife was Dutch, and every time I went home, she'd have gone home to her parents with my son, and he couldn't even speak English. I'm looking at this kind of thing. I would go away for five, six, seven, eight months, and it was one of those things—that impending feeling of doom was justified."

"So we did the Polish tour, Germany, France, Spain, Portugal, Italy, probably about thirty dates," says Tonka weighing in with his thoughts on band's self-destruction. "Paul Gray came in and took Billy's place, because Billy had to go back; he was committed to a Talas thing. Paul Gray was going out with my old girlfriend. A mutual friend of Paul's and mine had said, 'If you need a bass player, Paul has just left The Damned,' and I said 'Oh, come on!' Then he said 'No, he's a really good player!' So I said to Phil, 'He looks really good, he plays good; in actual fact, he's a lot like Pete, only smaller.'"

"So Paul came over to Athens and we were doing three nights at the big sports arena in Athens and that's when we decided to call it a night. It was a riot. We didn't play very long due to certain things, Billy left the next day and Paul joined and we came back to England, which we had to do, because all the deposits were in, the machine was running. Switzerland, Austria, the other gigs in Greece, Yugoslavia, Denmark, Sweden, Finland and Norway were all cancelled. Some of us got thrown in jail. The record company had a fit. We up and left Greece and left two tour buses, three semis and two Range Rovers over there (laughs), and said to the crew, 'You deal with this. We're going home.' We caught a plane the next morning. I said 'Fuck it.' I'd had enough. Phil went straight into a rehab thing and we did the British tour, which some of *Headstone* (compilation) was recorded for, and decided that was that. But we were supposed to do southeast Asia... Hong Kong, Malaysia, Indonesia. Never happened."

I asked Paul if when all was said and done, anybody ended up with any savings out of all this touring, the record making, the radio play. "50/50," says Tonka. "We spent a lot. A lot of it was cajoled away. When the L.A. move came about, it was a mistake in some ways. Due to management stuff, you're in a cocoon and you think it's going to last forever and you're driving nice big Jaguars and have houses with pools and tennis courts. The biggest problem you have is, 'Where can I score?' You know, and nothing else is a problem, and you go, 'Well, this is the life; I'm a rock star living in Hollywood.' Then you realise fifteen years later, if only we had invested some of that money..."

What about the houses? Were they at least purchased? "No, they were all leased. Live fast, in a big way. The thing is, the publishing things were kind of sold up the river without us knowing. Which would really have been our bread and butter right now. When you get older, you get wiser. But I wouldn't have changed it for the world, except I would have hung onto the money, and been a little more motivated to stay in control. You watch Behind the Music, and it's the same story with everybody. You go 'Jesus Christ, them too?! Ha ha ha.'"

"He's excellent," laughs Phil, years later summing up Tonka, at this point in the saga leaving UFO for good. "I saw him in London last year and he hadn't changed. 'So, you're paying for the drinks, are you?! You're paying for the drinks!' As Welsh as they come (laughs)."

Also leaving the fold at this point is Andy Carter, who feels he exited the band on a high note. "I think *Making Contact* was quite a good album," reflects Andy. "The material was quite good and we had Hipgnosis back doing the covers. Because we had lost them, I think, for *Mechanix*. But I guess with the band the way it was, it never got promoted the way it should have done. You want to know something very strange? That last English tour I did with them started on my birthday, which is March 23, and the last date was on Phil's birthday, April 15. And we were the only two original members in the band. It was so weird, like somebody tried to tell me something. And a week after the English tour we just called it a day. It was sad, because it wasn't even like we went out with a bang. The tour was mediocre. Phil just wasn't doing it. Have you seen him recently? Oh man, he looks good, sounds good. The band is fucking blistering, man. It's just such a pleasure to be back in that band. With Pete in the band and Paul Raymond, it's just like it was; we're a little older, but you get up there and it just turns the clock back."

As he explains, Andy would be leaving the band shortly after the release of *Making Contact*, ending up in the family's plastics, or "perspex" business. "Yes, he's involved with it," says Paul. "He didn't want to go on the road with us. It's all ups and downs, going on tour (laughs). He was getting a little less serious in the end. Well, I suppose, he took being divorced seriously, as opposed to someone like myself who takes it like a rock star. With Andy it was like, 'Well, I've been divorced now; it's cost me money. It's time to... do I really want to go on tour?' So your enthusiasm for music really isn't the same, is it? For me, it's what I do. Fortunately, I'm stuck with it. It's in my blood."

"Andy took over the family business, which has become quite a huge concern," says Paul Raymond adding a few more details to the Parker saga. "It's a perspex factory, a kind of plastic you see through. It was a small time concern and got really big. Once it was a joke in the old days, but now... Andy was the oldest son, and they said, 'You've got to take over the business; otherwise your younger brothers will take over.' He had to decide, 'am I going to keep playing with UFO or am I going to take the business on?' He had already gotten slightly out of the business anyway, and cut his hair off and put on weight and he'd not practiced the drums. I think he just saw it as a natural step. 'I'm done with it. I'm set up for life with this' and that was it."

"Yes, the famous Perspex Centre," muses Neil Carter. "In fact, Andy now is happily married again, breeding dogs and is doing the... you know, with the company car. It's very strange how we all end up. I am very, very happy with what I'm doing. I don't want to do it forever, and I'd like to retire in a couple years. I'd like to go live in Ibiza, actually. But at the moment I'm working off my whatsit, and I just can't believe I'm so busy. I never envisaged this at all. I'm far busier than I ever was in the rock music business."

Since these interviews, lo and behold, Andy has of course come back to UFO. Re-joining in 2006 for *The Monkey Puzzle*, Andy has now been back in the band for four albums of original material plus one covers record.

But back to Neil Carter for a moment, although here we are defining Neil Carter as an integral part of an important era in UFO, the man looks back on his very distant rock 'n' roll life and regards all that work he did for Gary Moore as more impressionable, memorable, something of which to be proud. Perhaps it's the reminding role played by the hardware, hardware earned, Carter says quizzically, by Moore in a metal role the legendary guitarist later disowned.

"It's very strange," muses Carter. "I'm sitting here looking at all my gold albums for all that stuff we did in those years, and I just can't believe that Gary dismisses the hard rock stuff. It's almost like... we had a chat a couple years ago about it, and it's like he's slightly embarrassed by it. Yet it set him up to do what he did. It paved the way for him to become... well, after we finished *After the War*, he went straight on and did *Still Got the Blues* and that's the album that actually pushed him into the next strata. But he was pretty big at the time that I was with him."

"The thing is, is that it never crossed over particularly. We toured America quite a few times, and Canada, but he never really made any headway in the States particularly. That's the difference between him and UFO, I suppose. UFO always did quite well in certain parts of the states. But Gary essentially did very well in places like Scandinavia and Germany, where UFO did moderately. But I've got gold albums from all those territories, really, really successful albums, but with Gary Moore."

"But for UFO? Nothing. I've got one silver album from UFO and yet I've got twenty-something gold albums for Gary Moore. Gary's stuff has done so well over the years. Like I said, 'Empty Rooms' has paid for my house; it bought my house. So it amazes me, that UFO has so much stuff over the years. But like I said, there has been so much wastage that has gone on. I see all these albums coming out. I walk into one of our record stores and there's this catalogue of UFO albums coming out. I don't actually know where the money goes, who gets the money. Because we certainly don't. It amazes me."

"The secret?" ponders Paul, when asked to sum up UFO's staying power, its solid and probably irreversible classic rock status, despite such "wastage" and resulting semi-poverty. "I would say determination and longevity and the chemistry in the band. Believe it or not, I didn't even realise it at the time. Later, with a retrospective look back, you go, 'I see how this works.' When you think about them being together since late 1969, and Michael getting into the situation in 1973—and I wasn't in the situation in 1973 but they knew of me, and then I wasn't back into the band until 1979—it's an incestuous thing, you know? That these people are drawn together all the time."

"It's not that, 'well, we've got to get that guy because he knows the stuff.' Because there are thousands of guitar players who could just slot into this situation. The personal chemistry was something that came across on stage quite well. You should see us in the live in Germany video. The guy with the camera is right up on my fingers and when you look at it you go this is why the band was good. I can remember the gig as if it happened last night. You talk to Dimebag or Vinnie or Marty Friedman or people I know around here, they come up to me and say, 'I saw you and you guys kicked ass.'"

"You look at bass players wearing stripey pants, Steve Harris and Brian Wheat from Tesla and Nikki Sixx. Nikki came to a gig for Waysted and told Pete that when we played a gig at the San Diego Sports Arena in 1981, Pete smashed a Gibson Thunderbird to bits on stage, completely gone, but the strings and the body were still hanging on and he threw it into the crowd and there were 9000 people there and Nikki Sixx fought everyone in the crowd and now he has that bass hanging on his wall over the fireplace."

"So it was that kind of thing. It was a big influence. Lars Ulrich or

Geoff Barton, the old editor of Kerrang!... it meant a lot, and the reason it was like that is because we would work relentlessly. We would tour and tour. When we arrived in a city, they would know about it, it would be wild, it would be absolute fucking mayhem. You look at the Behind the Music specials, Mötley Crüe, Bon Jovi, and it was like that, but going back to 1980, 1979, especially if we were in a place for three or four days."

And where was the blond German during all this? Well, eight months after the release of *Making Contact*, Michael was back with the fourth MSG studio album, *Built to Destroy*. "Great songs, shit production," says vocalist Gary Barden, returned after taking the third album off. "At the time, the whole band was actually hamstrung by the budget, so we couldn't pay someone like a Nevison or anybody else—the band actually did it themselves in the end and that wasn't a good idea. I'm proud about the songs on there. There are a couple of naff ones, but the majority I thought was okay. The number one and actually the number two album, they were the best. Until the money situation took over and the management and all that sort of nonsense, actually it was a good time. It would be nice to actually turn the clock back; that was actually very good for me and him. But in 1984, everything turned a bit nasty. I love the guy, you know? He's like a brother. We're the same age, almost. But now, he's not come up with anything that's making my heart leap or my legs shake."

Indeed the *Built to Destroy* album carried with it a patina of despondency. In direct contrast to the explosive, triumphant hard rock of its predecessor, *Built to Destroy* often sounded like self-defeating dark pop. Still, the band was doing fairly brisk business as a b-level act, the record rising to No.23 in the UK charts. A second MSG live album called *Rock Will Never Die* was released nine months later—this would mark the end of a surprisingly stable and regular run of records for the Michael Schenker Group, Michael then ditching the thing, re-emerging three years later with a new MSG, The McAuley Schenker Group.

"Maybe *Built to Destroy* went down a bit," reflects Michael. "We produced it ourselves and we had management changes and it was re-produced by Jack Douglas. But then again that was one of the more liked albums by other people, so I don't know (laughs). It was fun to work with Gary; he was a nice guy. We had lots of fun together, but then towards the end in 1983, 1984, he got too drunk and things got sloppy, and I decided to finish it there."

Chapter Five
Misdemeanor

"Chucking ideas about over cans of fine English ale"

Entering his wilderness years, Phil Mogg proceeds to keep the UFO name on life support (much like Tony Iommi and Sabbath in the same period) with a string of line-ups none too particular about adhering to past style points. The previous and proud UFO had in fact broken up, apparently because Phil Mogg had, had a "nervous breakdown" on stage, back in the Spring of 1983. Phil revived the brand the following year, co-anchoring it with esteemed alumnus Paul Raymond, and adding Jim Simpson on drums, axeman Tommy "Atomic Tommy M" McClendon (at the time, still living with his parents in Stockton, California), and Paul Gray, incongruously from Eddie & the Hot Rods and The Damned, to replace the zig-zagging Pete Way in both physical appearance and stage physicality. In fact Paul was a carry-over from the band's "farewell" tour after Phil's break with himself and with preceding bassist Billy Sheehan.

Before we get to the next record in the UFO saga, Paul Chapman offers a glimpse into his work immediately following his involvement with the band, years marked by projects with top-flight players bubbling to the surface and then fizzling. But then again there was Waysted, an under-rated yet short-lived haven of raucous barroom rock 'n' roll for the likes of Tonka, Way and even for a spell, Paul Raymond and Andy Parker.

"When the band broke up, after the *Making Contact* tour, when everything went haywire, Neil and Andy and myself went into a studio outside London, a place called Newbury, but outside Newbury, in the country. We were there a month and Neil and I wrote six tracks, which we divided between us. I came back to Florida and he actually went on to join Gary Moore. We said look, it's pointless saying we both wrote everything. We said, pick three and I'll pick three. I said, 'Well, I'll pick the ones that I had more of an input on, and you pick the ones you did more on.' 'So Long' was one of my three, the song that went on the Waysted *Save Your Prayers* album. To be honest, I can't quite remember the other two. I have the whole thing on tape, from then. One of Neil's was 'Empty Rooms' and the other one was 'Murder in the Skies,' the Gary Moore tracks, which I contributed to as well—the riff in 'Murder in the Skies.' Anyway, we arranged it like that and good luck to you!"

"Not so long back, about eighteen months ago, I came across the tape that we did, the demo. We were actually thinking of asking Robin Zander if he would sit in on it. Because Neil said that he didn't think his voice was really good enough. He said, 'I'm not confident that I could be the vocalist in a band situation.' I said, 'Well I am (laughs), because I think you've got a great voice.' Of course, when he went on to play with Gary, that's what he did. I mean, they split the vocals pretty much 50/50 between them. So I was right."

"I called him, going back two years ago, and he's living in Brighton now, around the corner from Phil Mogg and Gary Moore, of all people, all within like three miles, which is weird. He says, 'I keep bumping into them all over the place,' like in the grocery store. He teaches at a high school, and he's bald, squeaky bald. He shaved his head and he sent me a Christmas card. I was looking at this picture, and I was like 'Holy shit!' I mean, he's still the same Neil. He hasn't changed when you speak to him on the phone; he's a very gentle human being. But the reason I called him, was that I was trying to clean these tapes up because you can digitize this and that and take frequencies out. In actual fact, I can do it at the house here. I had an idea and thought it would be nice to do another anthology and actually include one or two of those tracks of me, Neil and Andy on them."

In actual fact, Paul ended up on the second Waysted album, *The Good the Bad the Waysted*, eight months after Pete, Fin and the boys had issued their stop-gap self-titled five track EP and three months after the final break-up of UFO. Why an EP? Pete Way explains. "We were going to do a tour with Iron Maiden and we didn't get the chance to go in to finish the new album but we had some songs that we had done and the full album wouldn't have been ready in time for the tour." The band at this juncture can be heard on the dodgy *Won't Get Out Alive* live CD released in '99 through Zoom Club, Waysted caught in action supporting Maiden in Cardiff in 1984, playing fierce, but unfortunately not recorded so well.

"I like them all in one way or another," reflected Pete, years later, on his Waysted catalogue. "I like them with each singer singing and of course with Paul Chapman playing guitar as well. They both have different identities to them. The other thing was that we were changing members quite a bit. It was one of those things where I had to think, if you were changing members, you can't keep telling people, 'Oh, this is the best line-up ever' and then you do it again and say, 'Oh this is the best line-up.' And then it naturally just fell into getting UFO back together."

"They're both different and they're both good in different ways," agrees Chapman, on the vastly divergent versions of Waysted. "I like the stuff with Fin because I like the sound of Fin's voice. But I had an issue with attitude with Fin. Anyway, I like the warmth and the way that, that album was put together, how we really pulled together as a team. I joined Pete for *The Good the Bad the Waysted* that year, when it was really him and Fin. Andy Parker was helping out and Neil Shepherd was playing guitar. We ended up doing the Iron Maiden tour, in Britain, which is why I ended up joining the band, because they needed somebody."

"It went from that to a full-blown, 'Let's do an album.' It wasn't even going to go that far. But the town in Wales where we did the recording was actually very close to my house, and it's an old studio that my cousin used to own. It isn't old anymore—a place called Rockfield. It was one of the first residential studios and the whole camaraderie of being in a band and living in the place together was cool and nice, and I think it reflects in the album. It was back in the days before everything began to go digital. We were still using tape. A lot of the things on there, you actually had to be very creative in the recording process, when you're only on a budget of like $20,000 or something. Liam Sternberg produced the record, and he's a fucking great guy and had some really cool ideas. Actually he was from Columbus, Ohio. He wrote 'Walk like an Egyptian;' do you remember that song? He had a couple of other hits. So Liam had a lot of creative input; he was like the fifth member of the thing. And Jerry Shirley from Humble Pie playing drums... it was very nice. Unfortunately we didn't tour with the album and then we ended up not playing with Fin. We were going to playing Israel and Fin wanted to rehearse for two weeks and we just didn't have the money."

A floated UFO live album from the *Making Contact* tour never materialized, although some intriguing live material from the British tour made it onto the "family tree" best of double album *Headstone*, issued August of '83, seven months after *Making Contact*'s release. Along with studio tracks from Scorpions, Wild Horses, Whitesnake, Lonestar, MSG and of course UFO, one could hear live rarities from the Chapman years such as "We Belong to the Night," "Let It Rain," "Couldn't Get It Right" and "Doing It All for You," along with a Chapman interpretation of "Electric Phase."

But back to business, a new UFO record did indeed emerge, in November of '85, and it was called *Misdemeanor*. For fans, it was closer to a felony, manslaughter perhaps, certainly a flagrant slander of UFO's goodly name.

First there was a single a month before the album launch, Phil putting forth the shamelessly poppy "This Time" for consideration. Catchy enough come chorus time, the bitter bad love song nonetheless lives or dies on a dated keyboard riff, not to mention clattery '80s production on the drum end from knob-twiddler Nick Tauber, who had worked with Girlschool, Stampede, Thin Lizzy and Marillion. The b-side was a non-LP track called "The Chase," which is a touch heavier but still cold and perky and poppy, making use of all sorts of disreputable '80s clichés.

"I came in after two weeks of disaster," chuckles Tauber. "We did another month and a half there at The Manor, and we ended up going to Hilversum in Holland to finish it off and that was okay. It's just that it was a lot of time together; it was long and stressful. But I liked it. I like UFO; they're a good band. Phil has got a great voice. He's got a real rocker voice, doesn't he? We were all a bit uncontrolled sometimes, but Phil was very good. He knew what he wanted to do and we got on with it. Still, it was a tough record. There was a bit of overindulgence, but I love the record."

"The only question is, I would have liked to have had time to mix it," adds Nick. "They went on tour straightaway, and I know that if we had mixed it properly, that would've been a bloody amazing record. The songs were great, the band was hot, the sound was good, we just needed to give it a fucking great mix. The mix was good, but it wasn't good enough. What managers and people do—and they don't do it now, but they used to do it—they'd book tours. I had it with Marillion. I had to finish the second Marillion album while they finished the tour. I don't like that. Because you should make the greatest record you should make. I know that we'd run over, but the UFO album, I took over from someone else, who they fired. So I was already behind the eight ball with that. But I liked them. Phil Mogg is an incredible singer, and charismatic as well. I enjoyed it. It's weird. I have a lot of people talk about *Misdemeanor* as a great record. I think it is a great record, but shrouded in a little bit of haze. A good mix would've cleared it up, you know what I mean?"

Once the album proper arrived (recorded at The Manor, mixed at Wisselord, in Holland), most press—if there was any to be had—focused on Phil's "hotshot" new guitarist, Atomic Tommy M, hyped, predictably, to be rock's next guitar hero.

"Atomic Tommy was great," remarks Tauber, "really, really good. It's just that because of their success before with Michael Schenker around the world, they were under pressure and when anything didn't work, they would always change it. I mean, that band is always forever changing. That's just the nature of the beast. Atomic Tommy was one of those classic... if Eddie Van Halen wasn't around, he could've been Van Halen, because his hammering technique and his speed was brilliant. He was an incredible player. It's just that Van Halen had done it, been there and done it. But his intonation, his speed, his tuning and technique were terrific."

"It all came together from Mike Varney, Shrapnel Records," sez Tommy, on getting the gig. "He had a column in Guitar Player magazine called Spotlight, and somebody should do that again (laughs). I submitted a tape to him. It all came about because I was actually plugging the band called Loudness, here in the States. It was the first tour they were doing here and I was the guitar roadie and my brother was the engineer. I was just calling Mike to tell him about the guitar player in Loudness, Akira Takasaki and say, 'Hey, this guy is really cool; you've got to listen to this guy.'"

"He said, 'Okay, but tell me about yourself,' because he had heard about me through a singer friend that we both knew, that he had worked with. So I said 'Okay, I'll send you something of my own.' As soon as I did that, he actually put me into the next issue of Guitar Player magazine, in his Spotlight column. From there, I thought this is really cool, because I was only doing solo things at the time, meaning writing songs, recording them myself (note: Tommy also had bands named Thunderwing and Boy Wonder). But I never considered myself a shredder shredder. I just write complete songs, lyrics everything. If there's a cool shredding thing in there, fine (laughs)."

"So anyway, he got a call, I think, from Phil Mogg," continues Tommy. "And Mike called me and said, 'Hey, Phil is looking for a guitar player to work with,' because the Paul Chapman version of UFO had just split up and he was looking to do something new again. So Phil actually came up to the Bay Area and I went over there to audition. There were a few other guitar players. We played four UFO tunes, the classic tunes, and then Phil said okay, and then he split."

"A week later I got a call and he said, 'Come down to L.A.; I want to hang out.' I think what he liked about me was that I wrote complete songs and I knew how to put it together. So I spent time with him and we hit it off and we actually went looking for bass players at the time. Because this wasn't going to be UFO. It was just going to be a new band, a new project that he was getting his teeth into, and he was looking for collaborators, writers, players. So we actually looked at bass players. Funnily enough, Jeff Pilson was one of the guys, which was right before he went into Dokken. So Phil went back to England and I waited a couple of months and then I got a call and Phil had it all ready including management to set it up, get rehearsal space and all this stuff. So I virtually just moved to England. Paul Gray was actually the bass player who did the last UFO tour before the split-up."

Phil talked generally about the difficult process of testing guitarists over the years, namely bringing in outsiders. "Yes, there were always different people considered, but nothing really went anywhere with anybody else. We were always a bit of an insular band. It was the people you grew up with and the people you played with. It was even a bit of a wrench when Andy left. I've always been a company man. I think it actually has a lot to do with growing up with Michael, Pete, Andy and the like, that getting to know other people is rather difficult sometimes. I remember going to see Yngwie, Steve Vai; I did speak with George Lynch, but we never got beyond that. It didn't really happen, plus they went off and did their own band anyway. But we were always one of those bands—it's better the devil you know. I don't think it's a great idea anyway to get somebody who is predominantly known. Even when Michael left and we got Paul Chapman in, we could have gone out and got some antsy fancy name, but it was better to have somebody in the band who was going to be a bandmate, a band player, somebody you knew. But I enjoyed playing with Tommy, lovely bloke."

"Ill in Athens? Yeah, ill," laughs Phil, looking back on the chain of events that led to his *Misdemeanor* booking. "I remember the theater but I thought, God, I don't want to go out. I was fucked basically. Absolutely, very fucked. I said, I can't do this. Tired and emotional and I'd had enough. Bad planning—a combination of people, being on the road, recording here, there and everywhere. It was like a spot in the gut and it got squeezed (laughs)."

And that was the aforementioned "break-up," after which, says Phil, he "went to the states for a chat with guitarists like Steve Stevens, Steve Vai, and Yngwie Malmsteen. Or rather, Yngwie had a chat with me (laughs). He wouldn't have been such a good bet for collaboration. But I liked Tommy's stuff and we were gonna form a band, not UFO, but it got turned into it." Of course, there was Paul Raymond. "Who you gonna call?" laughs Phil, "or, is it, the better the devil you know?"

"Not at all; he's gone through so many changes," bristled Phil, answering to comparisons with Black Sabbath in an interview with Rock Scene back in the *Misdemeanor* day. "I could see you saying that if we had kept going after 1983, because we probably would've done the whole musical chairs thing also. But there's a big gap between now and 1983. I spent a lot of time carefully getting this line-up together. I wouldn't consider it the same sort of thing, because this is a more stable situation. After the last tour, I packed up all my luggage and went back to L.A. to live. I really didn't have a clue about what I wanted to do. Actually I was just ligging around. I didn't have that much interest in music at that point."

"I bumped into Mike Varney in L.A." continues Phil, "who does the guitar spotlight for Guitar Player magazine, and went over to his place. We started talking about guitar players, so I asked him if he'd heard of any good guitarists. He's got loads of tapes from guitarists and bassists from all over the world, so he played me some tapes, and one of which was Tommy's. I thought it was really good, so he organized a jam session for us. When we played together, we got on fine, and by that time I was getting homesick for the stage. I wanted to seriously try and get a band together, but I didn't really want to have an all-American band."

"I went back to England and met up with Paul Gray," continues Phil. "Paul had some stuff written and we started working with that, and Tommy had some stuff written, so the only thing left to do was to try and get us together. We brought Tommy over to England and Jim came into the picture, then at the last minute Paul Raymond joined the band. After we got the band together, we did a tour to try and get a deal because we didn't have one at the time. During that tour we got a deal with Chrysalis... again! The problem with Chrysalis is that I don't think they ever knew how to promote us in the past. The situation this time around is totally different. There was a whole company change and now the attitude is different. Plus, we've got new management, so everything is more responsible and how it should be, rather than pissing out the window."

In terms of guitarists, there were actually two tapes given serious consideration by Phil. One was Tommy's and the other was Yngwie Malmsteen's. Malmsteen, of course, went on to form Alcatrazz with Graham Bonnet, the vocalist known for his work on Rainbow's *Down to Earth* and *Assault Attack* by a certain Mr. Schenker and his MSG cabal— both are classic albums, possibly the very best of those two respective catalogues.

"Well, that's a funny story actually," recalls Yngwie, on the heavy metal musical chairs at the time. "I was gigging with Steeler around town, L.A., San Francisco; we did the club circuit. I started creating a big buzz around L.A. Everyone was talking about me. 'Oh that kid's playing like no one else.' A lot of people were blown away. So I had a lot of people come and check me out. Ronnie Dio came around a lot—we became good friends and still are, although I don't see him that often. Phil Mogg from UFO was there, and a lot of other people I don't really know about. Phil said, 'I'm trying to reform UFO; are you interested?' I'm like, 'Yeah, fuck yeah!' I love UFO; I thought they were great. He says, 'Come over to my house tomorrow' and I said okay."

"I lived with a friend of mine, because Steeler lived in a really bad place so I slept in this guy's house. I got a phone call in the morning, and it was from Graham Bonnet's manager, and he said, 'Come down and check this out.' So I had to choose between Phil Mogg and Graham Bonnet the same day. So I went to play with Alcatrazz, although they weren't Alcatrazz then; they weren't anything. They didn't have a drummer, didn't have any songs or a band name, nothing done. Anyway, they liked me a lot and I liked them. But I went to see Phil Mogg, and he was at the time, really drugged-out or something; I don't know the story. But he definitely seemed like someone I couldn't work with. So I said to Graham, 'Okay, I'm in.' I already had a bunch of songs, and then I started writing more. So I basically wrote the whole album. I was not supposed to be anything more than the sideman. Graham Bonnet was supposed to be the star, but then I took the show over (laughs). Something happened there, I don't know, and then the friction started and they weren't all that happy how I stole the show. I didn't mean to. I just did what I did. So that's when I decided to leave. I just wanted to do my own thing."

"I'm obviously very pleased with the band the way it is now," said Phil, hitting his press rounds immediately post-release. "One of the keys is that we all work together very well. As our fans may remember, that wasn't always the case. Having everybody happy and working for each other's good is the only way to succeed. We had enough problems in the past. We want to make everything easy this time. In the past, we didn't have much willpower, and even less won't power. But hopefully we've learned our lesson. I'm not saying I'm drinking tea all the time, but I'm not going to go on stage drunk anymore either. There's a fine line between what rock 'n' roll is and what acting unprofessional is. I owe it to the band, the fans, and myself to make sure I can give the best every night, and I'm determined to do that."

"Hell, in the old days, we were all just drinking buddies," continues Phil. "Now we're a rock 'n' roll band. Tommy is a brilliant player. We've had a German guitarist in the band, an English one, and now an American. Each has been brilliant in his own way, and Tommy holds his own in comparison. He's a very distinctive instrumentalist who has a very definite West Coast flavour to his playing. Actually, we've shifted the balance between keyboards and guitar a little on this record, but the guitarist is still at the centre of what we do. We have a very rich tradition to live up to, and I don't think the fans would put up with us if we didn't have a guitarist who could be really amazing. That's a big part of what UFO's all about."

In official label press at the time, Phil circled the wagons, exclaiming gamely that, "the line-up we have today works together well, and believe me, that's so important if a band hopes to make good music. In the past, we had a very volatile group of musicians who often enjoyed lifting a few pints at the local pub as well as going on stage. We still like to have fun, but I think we are a little more serious now. We know that this unit has a lot to offer, and we don't want anything to stand in our way. We've grown tremendously with this record. We've brought in a bit more keyboard and we've tried to make music as contemporary as possible. I find it a bit offensive when bands who had success in the past just try to use the same formula over and over again. If you have talent, there's room to grow while maintaining the same elements that first made you successful. As well, playing live has always been a big part of UFO. I'm really looking forward to playing the new material in concert because quite simply, it's some of the best we've ever done. If people liked us in the past, I think they'll have no trouble with the band now. UFO will always have something special to say."

Indeed to all with ears, it was readily apparent that keyboards played a big role on *Misdemeanor*, and that in fact, the guitarist wasn't central to *Misdemeanor*. Fans noticed instantly, as did Atomic Tommy himself. "Paul Gray had a punk background but he wrote a lot of stuff and he actually wrote a lot on keyboards. That's why the *Misdemeanor* record had a big keyboard-type sound. Even though Paul Raymond played it, Paul Gray had actually written a lot of parts." Nor did his work go uncredited—Paul Gray is cited on five of the album's ten tracks.

Asked by the author more that thirty years later how much he liked the *Misdemeanor* album, Gray says, "Not very. I don't like the record. Well, I like the record, but I don't like the production on it. The production was just... it wasn't good. But I loved being in UFO. They were really, really nice guys. Phil Mogg, I got on with like a house on fire. Very fun time. You know, we had five years of immense fun."

"It's a shame the album turned out like it did," continues Gray. "There are various reasons for that, that I won't go into. Not the band's fault, I hasten to add. But I've still got the board mixes, and they are so full of spirit and energy. Then somewhere down the line it all got thrown out of the window. But it was good fun. I still go to see Phil from time to time, go and have a beer with him and everything. So, it's great and they're still going. People say it was a strange band to go and join, and maybe it was, but the funny thing was is that I never changed the way I played with the band, to be honest. Quite a few the songs that ended up on the *Misdemeanour* album, I'd written for The Damned. But I'd left them before they could ever get recorded. So it just goes to show that, had they been with The Damned, they'd have sounded very different to UFO. The riffs are still there and they're slower, and the choruses are still there, but of course they've got a totally different top line and singer."

So "This Time," "Night Run," "The Only Ones," "Blue"... some of these could have been Damned songs.

"Yeah, "Blue"... and "Night Run," was actually pretty fast. Yeah, when you get in a room... you see, this is what can make bands so unique. You can take your songs or your chords and riffs to one band, or one bunch of people in a room, and you go in with a bunch of people with the same riffs or chords the next day with a totally different bunch of people and it will sounds totally different. That's the great thing about being a musician—if you're flexible. So there's no "I want it like this, gotta sound like this.' You just chuck it out there and let the individuals in the room make with it what they will. That's when the magic starts happening. With UFO, there's lots of stuff that ended up not being used as well. We did a lot of songs for that album as I had these germs from doing stuff with The Damned. But those songs are probably influenced by the other stuff I was listening to at the time. It's never conscious. Whatever you come up with, that's what you chuck in the pot, and people either like it or say you've totally lost the plot (laughs)."

Asked to sum up the undisputed leader of the band at this point, Phil Mogg, Gray says, "Phil is a great lyricist and he's a phenomenal singer. When we were demoing it in my house, before that version of the band got together, the hairs on my arms in fact would literally stand up. He sat next to me singing and I thought, this is extraordinary and he gets it. He'll go through ten song ideas and he would just suddenly stop and he'll sing. He'll know that's the one, and his melody will remain pretty much unchanged up to the actual record. But he's very spur of the moment. What sounds right on the spur of the moment will often end up on the record, or inform how the lyrics are gonna go. He spends a lot of time on his lyrics, and like most vocalists and lyricists, they're not always finished on time (laughs). So you wonder what the finished thing is going to be like. But he was great to work with. We spent hours and hours shut up in my music room chucking ideas about over cans of fine English ale and having a laugh. Yeah, got on great with him. It's lovely that they're still out there doing it.

"Come to think of it, now that you bring it up, yeah," figures Tommy, on whether there was label pressure to make the *Misdemeanor* album so keyboard-laden. "Because that's what was going on in America with Night Ranger and some of that stuff. So I don't think it was intentional to be commercial but I think the label really didn't know what to do with us. We wanted to be hard rock and heavier but let's pick the songs that are a little bit lighter, kind of thing, for release, as singles and whatnot. I can't remember what the single in America was; I don't think there really was one. Chrysalis was starting to fold as well. It might have been 'This Time.' We had 'Night Run' which we always preferred performing on TV shows and stuff in England but 'This Time' was actually the single release, which was more keyboard-orientated."

I wondered how much of a UFO fan Tommy was prior to joining up with the boys. "Oh no, I was actually a MSG nut," chuckles Tommy. "I was totally familiar with UFO and had a couple of the records, but not every one. But as a guitarist, I would follow Schenker. Oh, he's doing MSG now, let's check that out. I know a lot of the people who come to see us remember us when people like Michael Schenker and Paul Chapman played guitar in UFO. They want to see if I can match up. Well, I don't feel I have to take a back seat to anybody; I play my way. I'm not trying to copy their styles. Even when I play a few of the older numbers in concert, I bring my own attitude to them."

Was the audition a cattle call? "No, no cattle call at all. Sure I was a little nervous. He sang and everything as well, so that was really cool. What he did is assemble a little band so there was a drummer, bass player and another guitar player and you all just got together and played these tunes and he sang."

"Both are very gifted but very different," notes Paul Raymond, comparing Tommy to Paul Chapman. "Paul's playing was more my cup of tea, more blues-based, more raunchy, and he had a fantastic stage sound. He was an effortless player, even with a bottle of CC in him; made no difference—he always sounded bloody good. He just did it: Excellent bassist too—A consummate musician and great fun to jam with. Tommy was a great American player, I guess. It's a personal thing, but my favourite players have always been rhythm-based—Kossoff, Townsend, Rick Nielsen, and yes Schenker—and I guess Tommy was more a part of that American guitarist thing in the '80s of what I call wibbly wobbly playing. I didn't warm to it as much. But that's absolutely no reflection of his ability, just my personal preference."

"Actually Phil became very responsible," laughs Tommy, recalling his time making the album and touring. "It was great, some of the best times I've ever had in my life. I wasn't particularly fond of living in Birmingham, England and neither was he really; he's a London guy. But we were there because that's where the management was and that's where they could take care of us. Phil was great, always fun, never a dull moment. Paul Raymond is great too, still a friend. I don't get to talk to him very often and he doesn't have email (laughs), but I love the guy. He always can make me laugh. Pete Way, I didn't see much of. At that time he was in Waysted. I did actually see him a couple of times. We went to visit him in the studio in the country in England, and he actually came to a couple of gigs when we were somewhere, possibly Denmark. He's a sweetheart."

As for the band's pretty much unknown drummer, Jim Simpson... "He played in... now you're making me think... Magnum. Before that he played in a local Birmingham Beatles-influenced pop band called Bloomsbury Set, but he was a rock drummer and he played in Magnum and then from there he came to UFO in May '85 (note: Simpson later moved on to Wishbone Ash and Skunk Anansie). We did a tour with another drummer first, Robbie France from Diamond Head. So yes, we actually toured first, in the UK, supported by Tobruk. It was like, 'Go out and tour and impress the record company that you can still draw' (laughs). It was one of those deals."

High points on the decidedly AOR-ish *Misdemeanor* were frankly few and far between. The aforementioned "Night Run," (Phil, befuddlingly mixing love lyrics with bad boy lyrics), was moderately raucous and moody, even if it's chopped at the knees by a poppy chorus. "Meanstreets"—with the exact same problem lyrically as "Night Run"— is total metal, of a middling type that would serve as frame material on '90s UFO albums like *Sharks* and *Covenant* and *You Are Here*, as is record closer "Wreckless," which nonetheless includes the most musical and memorable solo from our Japanese-American six-stringer Tommy. On the literary front, Phil paints an adequate picture of a hothead in motion, weekend coming, lots to do, let's go, girl.

"Heaven's Gate" inverts the "Night Run" situation by failing for the verse and triumphing with a strong chorus. Adding an extra layer of irony, the song would be the b-side of the "Night Run" single (red vinyl— neither of the record's two singles charted), launched three months after the full-length's creep into the shops, as well as the low end of the UK charts, at No.74. "Heaven's Gate" includes the biggest, fastest rip of solo guitar from the Atomic one. Best track on the album however is "Name of Love," a dark popster with a passionate verse melody and an urgent chorus. Amidst faux sophistication everywhere, this one track bleeds the real thing.

With regard to adjunct releases, there was also the UK-issued US remix EP, which gathered three Dave Wittman remixes—for "Night Run," "This Time" and "Heaven's Gate"—adding LP track "The Only Ones" (sourced as from the *Car Trouble* film soundtrack). Indeed the American version of *Misdemeanor*, released six months after the UK issue, featured these three songs in their remixed form, along with "Name of Love" and "Blue" (quite a good "love gone bad" lyric from Phil, that one), also remixed by Wittman. Differences are minimal.

On the record's cover art, a photo of a tattooed young girl holding a gun, Tommy offers that, "we were under the gun to just pick something. It was like, tour starts on this date, album is done on this date, out on this date, and that photograph came out of a photo book I believe that we all looked at and went, okay."

"We got the cover first," explained Phil at the time, who goes on to discuss the inevitable heavy-ing up of the album's tracks live. "When we were looking for a title for the cover, none of the song titles really fit, so we bantered about titles. Then one of the guys at Chrysalis' art department came up with the title and we said fine. Musically, I'm as happy as one could be for a first album. At present time, I'm very happy with it. It's difficult to say whether we'll stay with this sound until we actually finish this tour, because as we are playing more live—everything is changing. The songs are becoming more aggressive to a certain extent. By the time we finish this tour, we'll be playing in a more hard rock sort of vein. That's the direction we're going in live, so maybe some of that aggression will find its way to our next album."

"So far, the songs we're doing are primarily new ones and they've been going over well. I suppose there are quite a few people who come to our shows expecting it, but doing all the old stuff wouldn't really do us any good. We don't want to rest on this band's past labels. This is a new band with new songs and we intend to keep it that way. We do some of the really popular old stuff and it goes down really well, but the newer stuff has been going down well too. I can't complain. There's a lot of people that have seen us over the years, but there's also quite a few people who haven't seen us before, like our younger audience. The old stuff is so influenced by Schenker that it really wouldn't make any sense for us to do it because it's not us anymore. The idea is to re-establish ourselves with this album and tour. We don't really expect anything drastic to happen, but if something good happens, great! We just want to re-establish ourselves and we are starting out on a kind of grass-roots level."

On the subject of wrenching a single out of the record, Phil had said, "That's all it needs. That's a fact of life. If we get one, fine. If we don't, that's fine also. When you get on the radio in England, it brings a lot of credibility to what you're doing. The public goes, 'Yeah they are good,' so it convinces a lot of people that what you're doing is good and worth the money. I think if we had a reasonable hit in America, we would have brought all the sceptics out of the woodwork. The Americans are into rock 'n' roll as pretty much a lifestyle. In Europe, it's like something you have to search for on the radio and press."

Touring for the album kicked off with an exhaustive thirty-three dates in the UK, with proggers Pallas and popsters Shy as support, highpoint being nicked as warm-up for Deep Purple's reunion show at Knebworth, follow-up leg being European dates with Accept.

"It was a fun tour actually," says roadie road warrior Graham Wright, known for his jaunts with Black Sabbath through the Ozzy years and into the Dio era. "We did some European dates and English dates and a tour in the States. It was a fun tour; we were doing theatres and clubs throughout America. It was actually me and Les Martin, who used to be Geezer's bass tech, and we were just looking after the back line. It was okay, you know. It wasn't like a big arena tour we did with Sabbath."

"During that year, Phil was pretty good. I never really actually witnessed him losing his temper. Pete wasn't there, of course. It was Paul Gray, who was sort of a Pete clone, a good guy. It was about twelve months I worked with them. Phil was looking after himself. He was trying to calm down on that *Misdemeanor* tour. He was trying to keep away from the Carlsberg Special Brew (laughs), a strong liquor, a strong beer—that was his drink. Halfway through the American tour, Paul Raymond left. We were in a hotel in Phoenix when he left. We were in one of the suites, and he had an argument or something about the music, a musical difference with Phil, and Phil says, 'Well, you might as well leave' and he left. It was like, 'Well, I'm going' and everybody went, 'See ya then, bye!' (laughs). Then we just carried on, without getting anybody as replacement."

As a family tree sideline to the tale, Pete Way, Paul Chapman and a couple of new guys were struggling to keep the fine Waysted legacy alive. *Save Your Prayers* arrived in 1987, and the sound was shockingly slick and accomplished, due to elevated production values and, as Paul explains, a smooth hair metal crooner in Danny Vaughn.

"I got Danny involved in the band, who was in the band I had in America before I went back to join Pete. So that's the Danny Vaughn connection for my second Waysted album. When we started recording *Save Your Prayers*, we did quite a lot of writing—obviously, we had a far better deal. We were with Capitol/EMI and we had bigger management. And Danny and Johnny (D, or Diteodoro – drums) had a different feel, being American, which was kind of okay. It made the album kind of high-tech glossy, which was really nice. Actually, in retrospect, when I listen to *Save Your Prayers* now, I really love it differently to the other one."

Producer Simon Hanhart was the other transforming piece of the puzzle. "That was an EMI/Capitol find," explains Paul. "He had just finished doing Marillion. Simon is a superb guy. In actual fact, he went into the record business as an executive after. He produced a bunch of albums and he produced my *Ghost* album, at Rockfield. He came down and did it for nothing, drove all the way down from London, like 200 miles—God love him, didn't want a penny to do it. I think it was like the last thing he did and then I think he got a job with Capitol or some label like Geffen, A&R head or something and I didn't hear from him for years. Then somebody just came into my shop with the new Asia album from last year, that was recorded in South Wales, near where I'm from and I know the studio. It says produced by Simon Hanhart. So he must be back producing again."

"Really, really good guy," continues Tonka. "He was young, bright, very, very clever with a good ear. There's a track called "When Hell Comes Home" on *Save Your Prayers*. The bass drum on that, it wasn't how it ended up. It's not what you're listening to. What ended up happening was—and I know, because I had the room above the control room, and he kept me up all night—Simon spot-erased every single bass drum, one bass drum in every measure of the whole song, and he replaced it in a different place, with a sampled bass drum from "Let's Dance" by David Bowie. So the bass drum in "Let's Dance" is now actually one of every three bass drums in every measure."

"Then he got Pete to play along with the bass drum. It was a new concept for Pete, to actually play with a drummer. Andy Parker would never even have him in his monitors (laughs). He's like, 'Don't put bass in there!' A bit of a funny thing and it changed the whole feel of the song. So yes, Simon actually erased every single bass drum and he dropped in every single bass drum in a different place and it took him thirteen hours or something. I mean, this guy... the patience. I was upstairs trying to go to sleep and I would wake up four hours later to go to the bathroom and he'd still be doing it. This happened three times. Yeah, the guy, when he got stuck into something you just couldn't... You know, if that had been me, I would've been, 'Aw, fuck it, leave it out.' But he's very diligent when it comes to stuff like that and he had a really great ear."

Chapter Six
Ain't Misbehavin'

"The money started running out"

With prospects at an all-time nadir, UFO limped back from their US club dates to record an EP called *Ain't Misbehavin'*, which was to signal the demise of the band for the second time in four years. As a side note, Paul Raymond did indeed eventually get replaced in the interim, by a mate of Tommy's; David "Jake" Jacobsen, who had worked with a pre-Mr. Big Eric Martin. However Jacobsen is not credited on the EP that followed the downscale *Misdemeanor* tour.

"Well, we got dropped from Chrysalis and actually the money started running out," recalls Tommy, on why *Ain't Misbehavin'* was only of EP length. "We all started doing different projects at the time. Phil started helping Nigel (Mogg, Phil's nephew) with Quireboys. Paul started doing something else. Jim started playing in a pub band and I started doing sessions. I also hooked up with Clive Burr (Iron Maiden drummer, since deceased, March 12, 2013 due to complications from his long-term muscular sclerosis) and we tried to start a band. We did quite a bit of writing. We tried to start a band so I ventured down to London quite a lot and we would get together. We didn't have a name; we were just writing songs on a four-track, based in a little basement he had with his drum set up. I know he has some health problems now but he's such a sweet guy. Every time I went there, I just loved to hang with him. I still have those recordings; they're just demos. We just sang them ourselves because we said, 'Okay, we'll find a singer and he'll sing these.'"

The EP, out on the mid-sized FM Revolver label (not issued Stateside), comprised six tracks. It was certainly punchier than the thin and high-strung *Misdemeanor* debacle. Opener "Between a Rock and a

Hard Place" could have fit that record though, with its pussyfooting verse opening to a churning guitar chorus. The track has the distinction of housing one of Phil's most mean-spirited lyrics ever.

"Another Saturday Night" was a signature power ballad, adhering to all the rules, adding tinkling keyboard and ooh-ooh back-up vocals. "At War with the World" was a more than acceptable snarling guitar rocker, even if the lyric was less than its epic title, being merely about catching her with another guy. Onto side two, "Hunger in the Night" was a typical hard-edged hair band rocker the likes of which Alice Cooper or Dokken might have done at that period, Phil turning in an edgy night stalker lyric that might stop at sex or then again might not.

"Easy Money" is equally guitar-strafed and chugging (Phil's lyric is a confusion muddle of motion), as is closer "Rock Boyz, Rock," more of a melodic though brisk party rocker, Phil's once reliable wordsmith skills on hair metal auto-pilot. Sum total, the songs aren't great, the lyrics are quite abysmal, but the production and performances are solid and professional. As well, Tommy gets an opportunity to shine and he doesn't waste it.

In closing, Tommy compares *Misdemeanor* to *Ain't Misbehavin'*. "The first batch was—what's the word I'm looking for?—it's like a balance between guitars and keyboards. The EP was definitely more guitar-based and we did that intentionally on the EP because we wanted a more raw edge and just let that develop and come out. Unfortunately it never turned into a full-blown album, but that's what it was going back to."

Meanwhile, with UFO floundering, six months previous to the release of *Ain't Misbehavin'*, Michael Schenker had emerged with a major label deal and a new MSG, the McAuley Schenker Group, fronted by the big-haired Robin McAuley.

"I was born in Ireland, moved to London at the fine old age of 19," begins McAuley, offering the tale of his time with Michael. "I then performed with a band called Grand Prix. There I moved on into Germany, and did a bunch of recordings and ended up doing the remake of 'Stairway to Heaven' with Bobby Kimball and the Far Corporation, which was a top five in England. That segued into my meeting with Michael Schenker. I auditioned, and I think I was the last of 17, or maybe 13. A great man once said, 'The last shall be first, and the first shall be last.' I can't remember his name, but I think he was really important."

Perfect Timing was issued October 12, 1987, through a deal with

Capitol/EMI. Joining Michael and Robin—only these two guys are pictured on the cover—are Mitch Perry on rhythm guitars, Rocky Newton on bass and Bodo Schopf on drums. *Save Yourself,* same line-up, shockingly, came out almost exactly two years later, October 10, 1989, this time with pop guy Frank Filipetti producing. Up into early '92, a third and final album arrived. The ridiculously titled *M.S.G.* album, produced by Filipetti and Kevin Beamish, featured a whole new backing band, namely Jesse Harms on keyboards, Jeff Pilson on bass and James Kottak on drums.

"*Perfect Timing* had some really cool tunes on it," offers Robin, asked for a contrast between the three records. "We weren't particularly happy with the end thing, the production. A lot of people say it's their favourite record, oddly enough. We deliberately kicked it up to a notch when it came to *Save Yourself.* Michael played a lot of great guitar stuff on *Perfect Timing* but it was a little off in the mix, more commercial, maybe? Our first outing together. But *Save Yourself,* I love that record. It's a little harder, where we really wanted to be."

"The third record became not necessarily a studio record—they were all studio records—but it was a different line-up on the record, with James and Jeff, very good friends of mine. Kottak came straight out of Kingdom Come, a band that I loved. I love his drumming. Jeff Pilson was actually the best man at my wedding (laughs). He's out with Foreigner now, of course. Great players, and again it was a different record, that we took out in an unplugged setting. It worked really, really well in both arenas, from playing full-blown to acoustic. But at that time, Seattle was closing in around everybody (laughs), and it was time for all of us to wrap up like mummies, as the industry, I think, wanted us never to be seen again."

"Oh my God, strange, yeah," laughs Robin, asked about what it was like constructing songs with the Michael Schenker of the late '80s. "In the beginning, we went into a small room in Hanover, Germany, and we treated it—and this is straight up—like a regular working day. We did a full eight-hour day. We sat with a little four-track Tascam at that time, and he would—or would not—have some very basic chord structures, or a series of different ideas, that would culminate into a song. The whole process was that we wanted to really knuckle down and see if we could nail a song a day. That's basically what we tried to do. It didn't always happen, but for the most part, the 95%, 99% of a semblance of a complete piece of work would actually materialize in an eight-hour day."

"Obviously, I would tweak lyrics and we decide we didn't like this, and he would change the melody or an idea here, but he never really worked on a guitar part or lead breaks per se until all the vocals would be done. Because he really loved to trade off on whatever the vocal melody does, because he does some great shit in between all of that stuff. As time went on, I was residing in L.A. before he was, and then he would send me ideas—I would get cassette tapes (laughs), so many ideas, bits and bobs, and I'd take snippets of one and attach it to another piece. I would basically put the arrangements together I thought would work better with a different chord structure, and we would get together and work again for hours, put it together, re-record it, chip at it again. It was a very interesting process. We always felt, it's funny, the song was the only thing that mattered, or was it a piece of shit? That's what we tried to do. Some love that stuff, some hate it."

Then there was the touring. Asked about fondest memories from those years on the road, Robin figures, "Well, when we did all the Whitesnake dates, that was pretty awesome. Def Leppard, in their prime, was just wicked. They had both *Pyromania* and *Hysteria* at that point and that was serious. Great guys; got to know them really well. I knew Vivian Campbell before he was even in Leppard, and great shame with Steve Clark, because he was a great, great guitar player."

"I really enjoyed the unplugged stuff," continues McAuley. "I know they always say that's up close and personal, but there was truly something very earthy about it. It was so bare bones. When people were doing unplugged, they were bringing out amps and orchestras, and I was going, 'Well, that's kind of unplugged.' We were two guitars and a tambourine. It doesn't get more stripped-down than that. And the sound came out pretty awesome and that's how we wanted it. We wanted to just see if we could do this really bare bones. I think if anything, all praise to Michael, Jeff Pilson came out for one portion of that, playing second acoustic, and then we had a guy from Shark Island, Spencer Sercombe, who is just a tremendous player. It was just great; you got to hear Michael playing almost Gypsy flamenco style, all those MSG solos that people had gotten to know."

"Michael is Michael," says Robin in closing. "He's a little unpredictable; let me just put it that way. But I think he was in a pretty good place. It's pretty evident on the *"Unplugged" Live* album, that, that was not a mixture of a bunch of different shows—that was one show. The unplugged was pretty consistent, so that says something about his state of mind at that time."

As a sort of fill-in project, Schenker was also part of the all-star Contraband project, issuers of a self-titled album in March of '91. Consisting of Shark Island's Richard Black on vocals, Vixen's Share Pederson on bass, Tracii Guns and Michael on guitars, and Ratt's Bobby Blotzer on drums, the band scored a bit of a hit with a slick, restrained cover of Mott the Hoople's "All the Way to Memphis."

Interestingly, Michael also gave a few guitar lessons during this time. "That was a period when Robin McAuley and I were waiting for our next record to be recorded and I had some time off—that's also why I did the Ratt project (Contraband). It was just something I did because I had nothing else to do. The thing with Robin... when I finished with Gary Barden in '84, I decided I wanted to have a partner. I felt comfortable to split things down the middle, not just financially, but also name-wise. It just so happened that his last name started with "M" so the band could still be called MSG."

As mentioned, the new band also sported a second guitar player, Mitch Perry. "That was also my idea," says Michael. "I always wanted somebody to support my playing. At that time, I was quite interested to see what it would be like to have a guitarist in the band who played totally different than I do, but still exceptional. There were two types of guitar styles that were popular at that time—one was more the Van Halen style, and one was more like my style. I thought it would be a good idea to combine those two styles in one band."

Chapter Seven
High Stakes & Dangerous Men

"I tried to keep the whole thing very straight and sober"

After a shared long exile, Phil Mogg and Pete Way returned from their long time apart in February '92 with the boldly titled *High Stakes & Dangerous Men*, a Castle/Essential-issued album that wouldn't see a US release until Griffin shuffled it out low key three years later.

In fan summation, *High Stakes*, recorded in the latter half of '91 at three different studios (always a bad omen with UFO), is lumped with *Misdemeanor* and *Ain't Misbehavin'* to form a sad batch of two-and-a-half records that pretty much don't qualify as UFO albums, due to the fact that the line-ups were tenuous at best to anything classic (ditto adherence to the UFO sound), and that none of them are up to scratch, even on wider scales of general rock 'n' roll creativity.

For this one, Phil and Pete called upon drummer Clive Edwards and intriguingly one of the hugely under-rated guitarists of the NWOBHM, Laurence Archer, who had distinguished himself through melodic hopefuls Stampede and later through Phil Lynott's doomed Grand Slam. Early rumours had the album title, tongue planted firmly in cheek, as *Laurence Comes Alive*.

"I'm currently working on material with Pete Way," Phil had said in the months leading up to the record. "There's more than a possibility that we'll put something out before the end of the year. We might follow up the US release of *Ain't Misbehavin'* with a bit of a tour. I'd like to slip in some gigs over here just to play. We haven't played out for quite a while. Pete's got continuously itchy feet. Pete and I just had a drink, sat down, and he stayed for a couple of days. We started playing and it went from there. We just started writing together again and said, well, should we do an album? We've got just over an album's worth of material. Some songs are "It's a Shame," "Electra Glide in Blue," "Borderline," and the other ones are called "Untitled," "Don't Know" and "Haven't Got a Clue"."

"Right now Atomik Tommy is not a part of UFO," continued Mogg. "Paul is down in Florida doing his thing down there. I think he likes the sun and he seems quite happy. The million dollar question is who will play guitar? The drum problem looks solved, and it looks like it's Andy Parker. Hasn't the eternal UFO problem always been, 'Who's going to play guitar?' The UFO line-up with Michael, Pete, Andy, Paul and myself was quite volatile; it could explode at anytime. Everybody had a say in things and probably the main problem with that band was that I had the biggest mouth. But the last version, Tommy and bassist Paul Gray, there were no great arguments."

Phil went on to say, when asked about the demon drug and drink, "I'm one of those people who fall into that category of persons where if someone asks, 'Ya want to do so and so?' I go, 'Well, yeah, okay.' Now I'm nowhere near as severe as I was then. I'm quite together."

"I think that's a good album, a very good album actually," says Pete, defending what many fans feel is the indefensible, although to be fair, the press at the time was not that bad. "There are some very underrated songs on it, or songs that never really got the spotlight. In actual fact, we're probably going to do a UFO DVD (this chat took place in late '04) and we were thinking of taking obscure songs, songs we haven't done together. Because obviously, when we worked with Michael, you tend to do songs you did with Michael. You wouldn't ask Michael to play somebody else's songs. But working with Vinnie and Jason, there are certain songs you go, hey, I want to try this and see how it comes out. Because UFO is actually very good and can stretch boundaries these days. So some of the songs on *High Stakes*, nobody much got to hear them, because it wasn't perceived as real UFO. It was me and Phil, but..."

"The only reason it was done was because it was good," said Pete at the time. "I came up and stayed with Phil and ended up staying for ages. We started getting ideas for songs and we talked about the things we thought we didn't do quite as well as we could have done the first time." When asked about the money angle, Pete said, "I don't know. Money is obviously very important, but at the moment we spent all the money doing the dates. In actual fact, we don't actually see a great deal of the money. We basically reinvested. You've got to reinvest."

In the same interview, Phil was asked why there hadn't been any vestige of UFO for quite a few years, up until this point. "Because there was nothing worth doing within that framework. It was even a no-no when Pete came around, but it sort of moved in that direction the more we got involved, and it seemed a lot easier than it had been previously. All the aggravation wasn't there. It was wanting to do it, rather than having to do it. We started knocking around with different guitarists, different drummers, which seemed to go on for an eternity. One thing that we didn't want was an Americanization of it. We wanted English guys and to keep it very London-based with no complications. I think we were looking for a situation where we could just go out and play, to squeeze out the other side and bring back the enjoyment."

On landing on semi-indie Essential for the record, Phil mused that, "it's one of those things, if you think and think about it, you get so worked up and it ceases to be fun. I know what you're saying, but hopefully they can pull one out. The options that were open to us weren't hugely great anyway, because the reputation isn't particularly good on some levels. It's like; 'They're a bit risky,' which is probably true. That's one of the reasons we went straight out and played live. If we were going to do anything the only way to do it is up there on stage. That's how we originally started."

And UFO never stopped trying to get Schenker back in the band. "There's been a few things going around," says Phil. "Michael's said a couple of things in interviews. We tried, way before Laurence and everything else, to try and find some common ground, but there was money being bandied about which was absolutely ludicrous. If Michael came in and we had two lead guitars, with Laurence, it would be a very hot band, there's no mistaking that. Whether or not it would be progressive from a musical point of view, I don't know. It's kind of an unknown quantity. The only way around that is maybe we'll meet up, have a play and see how everybody feels. But we've got Laurence to take into consideration and we certainly don't want to screw up what we've got at the moment, which is a very nice working unit just on its first album. The only thing we tried doing with this album was to knock out a load of overdubbing, the Leppard harmonies—we didn't want any of that. I can only write in one direction anyway. It's actually the album that I can play without cringing. It's only vocal stuff that usually makes me cringe, but there's a bit in 'Only You Can Rock Me' which goes 'I've had enough now of school and stuff now'... I'll have to change that one day."

"Nice guy, he was good," adds Pete on the accessible yet technical Archer. "He had worked with Philip Lynott. Ironically enough, I'm mixing the Waysted album with Robin George, and Robin George was the guitar player that had just joined Thin Lizzy when Phil died. And we were talking about Laurence the other day. You know, good guitar player." Pete adds that Clive Edwards "played with Wild Horses, Brian and Jimmy's band. It was just one of those things. People that worked together. You know, people working in London... who is going to work well with you, you know? You always did, going back to the original days, when people used to meet together in the pub and they'd go, 'Well, so and so hasn't got a band; let's form a band!' like over the weekend."

Speaking with Marko Syrjala in 2007, Pete framed the reunion with Phil for *High Stakes & Dangerous Men* this way. "I was always in touch with Phil because we had been friends for a long time. I saw them go up and down. In fact the first Waysted album and *Save Your Prayers* went higher up in the American charts than the UFO one did. But then I saw Phil and went, 'Let's write together again.' When you've known someone since you were 16, you don't lose contact and you're always talking about things."

Asked for his assessment of *Misdemeanor* and *Ain't Misbehavin'*, Pete told Marko, "Well, you know, I think the direction wasn't really particularly special. If I listen to some of it, which I never really do, there are some good songs there. At that time, if you think back, record companies tried to get you to make a single. So what happens is you're not really being true to your music if you're changing your music to have a single, so everything has that sort of softer approach. It even happened with Judas Priest."

And so a reunion plot was hatched. "Yes, I had got divorced and was hanging with Phil all the time and then we just picked up a guitar and wrote a song in between the drinking and watching videos. It became important and went on from there. The *High Stakes & Dangerous Men* album isn't bad actually. There are some good songs on it, but it almost wasn't really a UFO album, because it's like the other ones in that gap—it wasn't a solid team of people. It was mostly me and Phil writing and Laurence Archer, who's a good guitar player, and of course drummer Clive Edwards coming in."

Production duties on *High Stakes & Dangerous Men* fell to Kit Woolven, who had worked with Thin Lizzy, always the first band one thinks of when comparing other acts to UFO. "Excellent, Excellent," recalls Pete. "Kit, funny, *High Stakes*... if you go back to the Mogg/Way stuff and some of the Mike Varney things, Kit does a by far superior job to that. He catches a certain mood. It's just a shame in a way that we didn't work with him with what would be UFO. Apart from the fact that Ron Nevison was the next member of UFO, working with things, nonetheless Kit Woolven did a very good job."

The album would be recorded at a number of local studios from August through the end of December 1991, namely Livehouse Studios, Cornwall, Studio 125 Burgess Hill, Wessex, E-Zee Studios and Black Barn Studios. Don Airey would guest on keyboards and Terry Reid and Stevie Lange would provide extensive though sporadic backing vocals.

Instantly, upon opening track "Borderline," one hears the bluesiness of Archer set against production values that are incongruous with the energetic traditional blues metal of this upbeat track. Drums snap but are drenched in reverb, but most definitely its rock without keyboards and no real hair band signals. Most definitely, however, it is Archer that is a big part of this one.

"Pete Way and Phil Mogg had been asking me to join UFO for quite some time," says Archer, concerning his arrival in the ranks of the band. "During that time period, I did some recordings, and I got Fin, who was in the band Waysted, to sing on some tracks. In fact I had a whole side-project going at the time that I was writing, and I got Fin to come in and record some stuff. That got Pete Way a little closer, on each other's radar, and he kept saying, 'We need a British guitar player; we need a good British guitar player, and you fit the bill.' That was the thing. He must've been going on for years, really, asking me. And eventually when I was in a position to do it, I agreed to do it."

"But you know, it was really good while it lasted. The guy's got completely dry. But it was a strange experience writing. I wrote nearly all of it, 95% of that album, and myself, Clive and Pete put all the backing tracks down. I sort of arranged them, with Phil's vocals in mind (laughs), but Phil didn't actually sing. Actually, we didn't know what he was going to do until we had finished all the backing tracks, and then he came in and put all the singing down."

"It was quite an odd way of working," agrees drummer Clive Edwards. "When we were putting it together, lot of the time it was just me and Laurence hammering away. Pete and Phil had gone to bed. A couple of the songs, "Borderline" and "One of Those Nights," had words, and I think "Burnin' Fire." Those are the three songs we did, I think, which got the record deal. So the rest had no words, and we recorded the album with no words, so all the songs had silly names—like "Back Door Man", called "Spooky" and stuff like that—and then after we finished recording and dubbing in everything it was like, 'Come on Phil, we need to put some words to it.' And then you'll get some phone call in the morning, saying, 'Phil did a vocal last night on "Spooky;" it's called "Back Door Man".' And "She's the One" was called "Docklands." So it was a really odd way of working. And at the time, you felt God, had I known he was going to do that, I wouldn't have done this, kind of thing. But over the years you forget about it and you just listen to it as if it was always like that. It was actually done as like a karaoke album."

Next up is "Primed for Time," and this one's pretty much metal and potatoes hard rock, simple chords, party music, in fact, quite hair metal but no nonsense. "She's the One" is a pop song with acoustic, and is introduced by Clive Edwards doing rim shots. This one's in that Bruce Springsteen/Bryan Adams/John Mellencamp zone.

"Well, the whole discussion with Phil," notes Archer, "when we started the writing process, was that Phil in UFO—just like Phil in Thin Lizzy—was a massive Springsteen fan as well. He always wanted to write songs more in that ilk, rather than the British sort of riff-orientated rock music, big power chords, big changes, the big power ballad and stuff like that. As a vocalist, it's probably a lot easier for a singer to sing over a nice chord sequence, rather than three or four riffs strung together. And I was very much in that vein as well. I was very much into songwriting and the melodic side of things. So that album went down that line a bit, hence things like "She's the One," "Borderline," "Love Deadly Love." There are three or four songs that are quite melodic on that album as opposed to being just rock riff-oriented songs. I'm not saying they're not heavy or powerful songs, but they're open, with a little more space for Phil to stretch his voice."

Suitably, there are synth and key lines here and there, even a bit of piano, notably on "Love Deadly Love." "Yes, Don came in and played some keys, but there was no real involvement. It was very much a session."

"Ain't Life Sweet" is in fact, a riff rocker, sounding quite Michael of sweet and sour melody and note density. But then it's back to Clive on rim shots and acoustic guitar. "Don't Want to Lose You" is more Springsteen-esque and roots rocking than anything on the record, and features some of these nice backing vocals referenced earlier. One could imagine Thin Lizzy doing a track like this as well, or at least Phil Lynott, given the range across his two experimental solo albums.

Says producer of the record, Kit Woolven, who has worked with both Phils, "Phil Lynott is certainly more poetic than Phil Mogg, inasmuch as most—if not all—of Phil Lynott's lyrics could be read as poetry and they always had a story to tell. There was always that beginning, middle and an end, which I don't know if Moggo always has that, particularly. But no, that album was good fun, even if it dragged on a bit. Because Phil hadn't written the lyrics, so it took quite a long time to get the lyrics out. But it was nice working with Laurence and Clive Edwards. It's just a good rock record, really. I've always been, to be honest, more of a melody person, personally. I do like very strong melodic rock. This is what I liked about working with Phil, was that his melody was very good. Both Phils, actually, Mogg and Lynott."

I asked Kit if the toxic twins, Pete and Phil, were managing to keep sober during the sessions. "It started out that way, yeah," he laughs. "I tried to impose, well, not impose, but lead by example by not having a drink in the studio. It's very easy for a studio situation to become a bit like a party, which is sometimes a good thing, if you can have a controlled party, with everybody feeling really good; it reflects in the music and it comes across nicely. But it's very easy for these parties to get out of hand. So I tried to keep the whole thing very straight and sober, do the day's work and everything else. Phil was doing very well there for a while."

Despite a whole pile of the album's credits given to Pete and Phil as a pair, Kit affirms Laurence's assertion that he put most of the songs together. "No, I don't think Pete was. Laurence did an awful lot. Laurence had written all the riffs; in fact yes, Laurence was very, very instrumental. Phil would stick his nose in. It was very hard working with Pete. Pete would keep sneaking off and coming back slightly worse for wear, which made getting his bass parts down, very, very difficult. Backing tracks were mainly guitars and drums. The bass parts were recorded... it took a very long time to record the bass parts. Very often, after Pete had gone to bed, I would sit up with an engineer and I would replace a lot of the bass parts myself. Because it had to be done (laughs)."

Mid-album, track six is another bluesy hard rocker, "Burnin' Fire" in possession of a chorus that evokes memories of Johnny Cash's "Ring of Fire." Elsewhere there are Stones-like back-up vocals and a solid, energetic performance from Phil. "Running Up the Highway" is more of the same, opening with swampy blues guitar but then rocking hard on chords stacked like pancakes. But it's all a little brown and underwritten, as is next track "Back Door Man," which is a semi-ballad not done any favours by the brash and technical production on it.

Explains Clive, asked for an assessment of how these songs were written, "Well Kit, the thing is that we started writing this up in London, and we got a bit of it down, and we got the record deal, and when we got the record deal they said, 'Right, okay, we're going to send you down to Wales to write the album.' They shipped us off for a few weeks, to this rehearsal studio. It was like a converted barn on a farm literally in the middle of nowhere. One of the reasons was to keep the boys away from the pub, kind of thing, with no distractions. There was a pub but it was dreadful. It was like a sheep farmer's pub in the middle of nowhere and the place was awful. It smelled of sheep shit, basically. So there was nowhere to go and you just carried on. They would go to bed early and we would carry on until one or two in the morning. When Kit arrived, it was the second week, so we had all the songs that myself and Laurence would just play during the daytime, when Phil and Pete were there."

"In fact, there's a funny story," continues Edwards. "What Phil would do, he would sing a lot of the same words to the songs. He would do his 'la la''s and his phrasing and stuff, and he would keep using the same words. There was this one line in "One of Those Nights," 'She tripped across the floor,' and he was singing that line in loads and loads of the songs, all the songs. And Pete said, 'Here, Phil, will she be tripping across the floor a lot tonight?' Which I thought was hilarious."

"So when Kit arrived, he came down with all his gear and set it up. He had a porta-studio, bits and pieces like that, and we would tape it so we could listen to the tracks. So we spent a couple of weeks working with Pete and Phil during the daytime, coming up with new ideas, and they would turn in early, and we would often work until quite late on the rhythm tracks and the guitar parts and stuff, and polish them up. Kit would record them and we would listen to them and gradually we had a huge big clutch of songs. We dropped a load, for the album. There were probably about four or five other songs which we never got 'round to recording."

Asked for his impression of who is playing bass on the record, Clive says, "Pete is playing all of the bass. He had to redo a lot of it. The main thing is we wanted to get the drum sound, and for that, we used the studio mainly for drums. Because it wasn't a huge studio, so we took a load of ambient mics and stuff like that. I'm not sure, but the back tracks, were done with a DI bass, and then afterwards, once we got the drum tracks down, then we would clear out and put up the bass rig, and then Pete would overdub his bass parts. To be honest, I wasn't there for a lot of the bass sessions. Once you've done the drums, you've had enough. You've done your bit, done a lot of work. You want to clear your head a little bit. You've done a couple of weeks working hard at rehearsing, writing, and then you've recorded the drum tracks and it's a lot of work, a lot of intense pressure, getting drum sounds and drum parts. The last thing you want to do is sit there and listen to Pete Way play bass on all that stuff. 'I've heard this track so many bloody times!' Otherwise you just end up hating it, or wanting to redo it. So it's best to get out of the way."

Back to the track list, "One of Those Nights" is another poppy rocker, with both electric and acoustic guitars. Phil is heavily into Springsteen mode over asset of dependable "Louie Louie" chords come chorus time. "Revolution" has a similar light touch of an arrangement and a similar Bruce vibe. "Love Deadly Love" is framed by a medium grade heavy metal gallop, levity added through Don Airey's honky-tonk piano. Finally there's "Let the Good Times Roll" which is yet another frustratingly uncommitted rocker, bluesy, Van Halen light or strip club hair metal, recorded with too much drums and not enough guitar, not that the riff is anything to write home about.

"I enjoyed *High Stakes*, which wasn't really UFO but good fun," Phil told *Record Collector* years later, summing up, but remembering the time using different methods of recall. "We went to Russia, absolutely brilliant! Night train from Moscow to St. Petersburg—yo-ho-ho all the away with the Sunday Sport girls and that extraordinary vodka you think is so normal, but after five minutes, you're suddenly on ship. I had a rather drab accident when we were miming, and Pete Way was pushing me 'round in a wheelchair, which is most unfortunate, 'cos he found it rather amusing to leave me in different areas of the airport (laughs)."

A few years later still, Phil commented that, "The album we did with Laurence and Clive, I heard it the other day, somebody played it, and I went, 'Blimey, he ain't one half of a player; he's got some really good licks there.' Some of the material I really enjoyed. I've no regrets there whatsoever. That album was going to be called *High Stakes & Desperate Men*, but somebody said to me, 'No, you can't call it *Desperate Men* because people will think you're desperate.' Oh please, give me a bleeding break."

And then there was delivering this unappealing tranche of songs live, limited, but yes, it did happen.

"We played several festivals where there were bands like Asia, Magnum, various bands similar to what we were," recalls Archer. "I'm trying to think whether we supported anybody. We did England, Japan, we did extensive touring in Europe, all of Europe. We did some of the far-flung European countries, Greece and some other places. We didn't get to the states. That was the next thing. We went to Russia, which was really the end of the band, because Phil got to drinking again, and consequently fell off the stage. I just walked away from it. The fact that it was being recorded for TV and was live made it all the worse."

Asked what it was like being part of a rhythm section, live, with Pete Way, Clive says, "Brilliant. You never knew what he was going to do. But he was great fun. I mean, he's such a showman. He's all over the place. It was always entertaining, and Pete, certainly in my era with him, he was a very solid player. He's not Jaco Pastorius or Stanley Clarke, but what he does, you can pretty well hang your hat on it. He climbs up the PA, he plays the bass behind his head and stuff like this. People might think he might make a load of mistakes—he doesn't. His timing is pretty good. He knows those songs. We never had any issues going out there and playing 'Rock Bottom' and 'Lights Out' and all that lot."

As for the state of Pete's health, circa the summer of 2011 anyway, Clive actually had an answer, because twenty years after *High Stakes*, they were still tight. "I haven't spoken to him for a few weeks, but he's been working pretty hard," explains Edwards. "He's taking lots of tablets and stuff to get himself sorted. I mean, when I saw him last, he was actually in a right old state a couple of years ago, when it all kicked off. I think coming out of UFO and not being well and everything else, it did affect him. He was really gutted by the whole thing, so that probably compounded his actual physical health. But over the last year or so he's been doing a lot, and he's been working on his solo album. I did a few tracks with him on that, and then he started working with Michael Schenker and Herman Rarebell and so he's got plenty to focus on. The low point was when he was doing Waysted and it was like, 'Oh my God.' I actually saw a YouTube of Waysted, and Pete didn't move and if there's one thing about Pete, it's movement. Pete Way doesn't stand still. Pete Way is like a whirling dervish (laughs). It was quite weird seeing this version of Pete Way. But then there was another video where he got up with Michael last year at Shepherds Bush, "Doctor Doctor," and there he was prowling around the stage again. So fingers crossed that he's on the mend."

Chapter Eight
Walk on Water

"I have been happy in both worlds"

After nigh on a decade of spurious UFO records, UFO miraculously patched things up with the esteemed Michael Schenker and fashioned a record that was (gasp!) better than anyone could have thought.

But before one writes a record like *Walk on Water* and attempts, against all odds, to tour it, one has to get into the right headspace. For the happy heads in the band, that usually isn't much of a problem. But for Michael, getting to this point necessarily included "drama," and yet drama that in actuality approached personal revelation.

"Well, it started off that I was supposed to be making an MSG album," begins Michael, making the circular trip to this place. "Let's see, they had approached me over the years a few times to rejoin, but it never felt right. I never really had a reason to do so. When I did my *Thank You* album, I ended up being rich. Just because of the *Thank You* album. I never earned any money with UFO or anybody. So I left the machine, because I thought, wait a minute, something is not right here. I left because the managers were taking my money, but never opened any new doors. I came to the realization that these people just keep taking my money and telling me stories about how there isn't any (laughs). I couldn't understand it."

"So I left the machine and put together this *Thank You* album, acoustic instrumental music, and then I went on a promotional tour, by Greyhound bus, 10,000 miles, throughout the whole United States. I just knocked on radio station doors without appointments, and asked them if they wanted to do an interview or not. I did that for a whole month, and when I came back home, I was over-flooded with mail and money and everything. So I realised that I was surrounded by rip-offs all the time and people were telling me stories and putting all the money in their pockets. So I had a new experience and new insight and I understood something new that I wanted to share with UFO."

"When they approached me, in that same time, I said like, 'Yeah, you know guys, you never earned any money either. I just discovered something and I think you deserve to experience the same thing with UFO.' So I suggested to them, do the same thing that I just did, which was to make an album and then sell it themselves. But the thing is, you can only do something like this if your main focus is not success or prestige and all of that. You have to be humble. My whole attitude with the *Thank You* thing was that, as long as I can earn enough money to be able to have a couple of sandwiches a day and a roof over the head, I'm going to be fine. Maybe I only need to sell three or four albums a day and I'm going to be okay. So it was a very humble request. But it turned out to be totally opposite. Which showed me it's pretty incredible how things work in life. You are humble and modest and then the biggest thing all of a sudden happens. If you are greedy and pushy, then sometimes nothing happens."

"So anyway, that's what happened. I discovered something that UFO deserved to be part of, and therefore I suggested that. So we made this album and tried to sell it ourselves. We did it, and I remember Paul Raymond walking around going, 'Wow, I can't believe it. For the first time in my life, I'm earning some money.' But then, it all went to people's heads and they were all getting weird. I don't know what happened, but I guess that it wasn't time for them to do anything like that."

On a separate occasion, Michael told this pretty darn interesting story the following way, filling in a bit of detail on the bus action. "In 1992 I started to get away from the business end of music and to be creative in all aspects of my career. I wanted my peace so bad that the roof over my head and enough to eat was enough. With that attitude, I went on a promotional tour with my last couple of thousand dollars on a Greyhound bus. Someone would make the call ahead of time and at the next Greyhound stop I would jump out. I had two guitars with me and two bags. Fans would pick me up at the bus station and take me to the Motel 6 or wherever I would be staying. They would take me to the radio station and I would do the interview and go get back on the Greyhound and go to the next town. The person that was making the phone calls would tell me where to go to do the next interview. I would just follow the road to whoever was willing to do an interview. I rode 10,000 miles on a Greyhound bus all over the United States."

"When I came home, it was all there and it was only because I had a healthy attitude. Someone tried to copy what I did but it didn't work. I found out that if I had the attitude of wanting to be back on the charts and making it big, then I would have never been able to experience that particular part of my life. Only with a humble attitude was I able to do it. It was one of the best times of my life. I was all by myself but there was so much peace. When I came home I was overloaded with mail orders. Overnight, I was driving a Mercedes SL and I had two houses— it was just like that."

"All the years I played with UFO and with MSG, everyone told me there was no way to make money in the music business. The moment I stepped out of that industry, I became rich overnight. Nobody in UFO made any money, but somebody did because *Strangers in the Night* was chosen at the 25th anniversary of Chrysalis Records as their main album. So that means that something has been fiddled about that has not been discovered. Someday, all of a sudden, it may be discovered what happened. Maybe it was meant to be that none of us should have had any money because we would not have taken the same course that we took. That is why I never really feel bitter about things. I was very depressed about the loss of my recording studio, but I was also very exhausted. I was happy to stay in bed for six months."

"If God decides that you deserve more, then it will appear," muses Michael. "If you need to have it to continue to learn and grow, and if it is something that you deserve to have, then it will be there for you. If there is something that you think you should have, but the universe thinks it wouldn't be good for your growth, then you won't get it. You only get what you need in order to grow. I am blessed on that level. I have lived in very simple situations and I have lived in really wealthy situations and I have been happy in both worlds. I already know that it doesn't really matter if there is going to be money or not."

As an interesting side note, at one point it looked like none other than Paul Chapman might have been returning to the band. Tonka explains. "When they went and did the *Walk on Water* thing, Phil came over to Florida, and we were going to reform UFO with me. I believe that was 1993, and it was almost put together. The first gig was set up in Germany and at the last minute Rudolph Schenker appears and pushes Michael into the thing via Phil. The thing was, I thought if I do this, I've spent all this time building up a clientele of people who I want to teach. These are all guys who were really good players and they're professional people and I enjoy doing it because I'm playing all the time and it really taxes my ability from a theory point of view and a physical point of view. I thought, if this thing goes down the toilet in six months, I'm going to have to come back and start this all over again. So that was in the back of my head and it was a blessing as such that it didn't happen."

UFO indeed did play the German dates of which Chapman speaks, as a sort of "paid rehearsal," a walk on the waters as it were. Pete Way was interviewed in the middle of the seven gig run, December 20, 1993, in Nuremberg, by Mike McCann, commenting that, "we had three weeks rehearsal, and up until that point, it's actually twelve years since we've all been together. We didn't know how it would go, but we found it very easy as though it was last week—at the first rehearsal. So we just worked through the songs every day. In fact, the hardest thing probably was putting the acoustic thing together of Michael's (note: guitar tech Paul Guerin filled in the sound during the acoustic segment). But we wanted to represent that in the show."

"That was just a one-off deal, to be honest," says Pete, when asked at the time about *High Stakes & Dangerous Men*, and its limited release. "It could've been an album with just Phil and I and a couple of people, but unfortunately we fell into the thing of people always saying, 'Well, it's you and Phil; if you don't do it as UFO...' Actually we're quite proud of the songs on the album, but we'd have preferred to have done them with Michael, Andy and Paul, because the way we work together, we develop sounds more than just say Phil and I. We just sit with an acoustic to work on stuff, and we take it to a band. Whereas with UFO, we might have an initial idea, we get into a room and start playing and everyone develops a sound together."

"We knew we had been talking for nearly two years with Michael," continues Pete. "So we were looking for the ideal opportunity to get together, not to try out as such because that's the wrong word, but we always want to do something with 100% efficiency, and really that's why we didn't want anything other than what we consider to be UFO, this band, coming out. Also we would tackle record deals and that very carefully, because we figured that at this point in our career, we want everything to be absolutely right. It sounds a bit corny, but we have learned through a lot of mistakes in the past, because you can do something that comes out as only 50% of its possibilities. We figured that these seven shows in Germany were an ideal opportunity for everyone to feel comfortable, because we all live in different parts of the world. Michael actually lives in the States, I live in England and Copenhagen—my wife's Danish—Andy lives in England or Los Angeles and Paul Raymond lives in Tokyo. So just putting the whole thing together and finding a base is difficult."

When asked about Paul's Paul Raymond Project, Pete explained that, "he does it in Japan, the big planning and stuff. It's a lot harder to break, to take something out and send it over from Japan. While this project will take everybody's time when it's up and running, you know, everybody has interest in doing other things. Whereas Phil and I, to be honest, felt we didn't, and we didn't want to be forced into a situation of doing another UFO without the people that we feel is the band."

Pete adds his take on the thought that Paul Chapman might have gotten the nod for the reunion, the interviewer reminding him that Paul's name was even on the tour posters for the Germany run!

"Michael had been talking to us about doing something. These shows were offered, but we didn't know if the whole thing was going to come together. We'd spoken to everybody and Michael was going to get back to us. Basically it was just up in the air, and we had been speaking with everyone involved with the band. We are quite friendly with everyone now. So speaking to Paul, it was like, did he want to do some writing? He asked if we wanted to go to Florida where he lives. Obviously the idea was that we wanted to work with Michael, and that was that, but it had been mentioned perhaps doing it with Paul, and then work with Michael after that."

"Fortunately Michael said he'd do it," says Pete. "Obviously we prefer working with Michael. Paul's a friend, but this is the band we wanted to tour. Also, when you agree to do something contractually, and you don't do it because your guitarist isn't there, we could've ended up in a lot of trouble. So Paul was very much in between the situation when we didn't know if it was going to come together with Michael. What it is, is it's just different guitarists have different ways of doing it, I guess, with the amount of quality in their approach. Michael could come up with some really quality things at times, but I must admit some of the MSG things I didn't think were that great—certain great moments perhaps. With Paul, he was a safe bet in that you could make things sound good, but we never had what I felt were great moments. Don't get me wrong about that with Paul, but if you had to look for what made it tick or made people go and buy it, then it was probably created by some of the magic moments with Michael."

Pete went on to consider the possibility of working with Ron Nevison, which actually eventually did happen. "Ron would always be considered, but we don't want to be too much like memory lane, so there are certain ways of doing things. Ron's great, and I always like to work with him. Having said that, we'll have to look at the situation and try get the best available. Also, we're looking at the money because unfortunately we have a very tight budget, but obviously with the right record deal, we can have a closer look. We actually got Ron when he was engineering things for people like Led Zeppelin and Bad Company. We looked at things like that and thought that if he could get those sorts of sounds, he might be good to work with. So we're actually looking at Ron or somebody of that quality to give a new edge to things."

Finally, Pete comments on the demise of his Waysted project. "Oddly enough, that was a very similar situation to this in a way. When we started to change members, it got to the point where I didn't want the responsibility of the band, because you've always got to worry about who's getting what money, and paying this and paying that. Really, the whole enjoyment was going out of it, and I would rather have been able to go and play in some clubs or something with the band, and not have to worry about overheads and record deals. The actual thing of going on the road and touring the USA—if you're going to replace him with someone else—it all became a pain."

"Whereas with this band, at the moment, it's all good fun. It all might end in Hamburg (laughs), but seriously, this is everyone's enjoyment. With Waysted, Johnny was good—he played with Britny Fox afterwards—and Danny had that band Tyketto. I enjoyed it but at that point it started to get too serious, because you can't just put five people together and make a band that is a great band.

"Now with this line-up of people, we've sort of got five individual people that gel together and actually enjoy each other's company," says Pete, back to the present situation with UFO. "I feel that this is a good band and that's only after three shows. We thought we would have to really work on the songs, but as soon as Andy started playing and I played to him, the feel of the back rhythm section with Michael's guitar over the top really began to build. So hopefully by Hamburg, I'd like to think that the whole thing would be absolutely awesome. We're really enjoying it. I think that, plus the fact that Michael hasn't played electric for nearly three years onstage, and basically it's his band. When I say it's his band, it's my band, Phil's band and Paul and Andy's band. It's like when he had MSG. In theory, you've got a lot of responsibility that perhaps you don't want. Whereas when you can filter five people's energy into one thing, then it's the band's responsibility."

Alas, drummer Andy Parker, returned from a long exile, would only last through the making of the album, with journeyman Simon Wright taking over for the combustible tour dates.

"The whole thing was weird," begins Parker. "I'd just moved from California. I had moved back to England, taken a job with my family, a factory job, and I got this call. They'd been calling me over the years all the time. 'We're going to do this, do that, get the band back together,' like the Blues Brothers or something. 'Yeah, yeah, whatever.' I'd just made this huge life choice to go back and work with my family, from California."

"All of a sudden the Japanese put up this money, and I get this call, 'We're going to make this album.' So it was like, okay, I hadn't seen the guys in ten years, Michael even longer. He left in like '79 or something. I think I left in '83, and Paul had done the last four years. And I hadn't seen any of these guys, maybe talked to them on the phone or whatever. But Michael is so good. I'm gonna tell you one thing, and I don't tell this to many people. He's the only guitar player—and I can't remember where the show was—but I remember that we were playing and he was soloing and his solo was so amazing that I stopped playing. I kind of lost it because I was listening to him on the monitor and that tells you just how good the guy was. So, fine, I wanted to do this, and I had to negotiate with my brother to actually get the time to go and do it. I didn't know where it was going to end up."

"So I just took my whole vacation for a year, went back to California where I had just moved from. I had just been living there for twenty years, and then moved back to England to make an album. It was cool really. Musically it was great. The guys had some stuff already, some good ideas, and we went and rehearsed for a couple of weeks, three weeks maybe, and then into the studio."

"I think I actually recorded everything... because I was on a time crunch. I had to get back to my job, or had to make a decision to quit my job. But I just couldn't do that long distance, go away to California. My wife was in England and we'd moved there, all our belongings were there, and the whole thing was a bit bizarre, that it all finally happened when I moved back to England."

"So we did the album," continues Andy, "but for me, what I noticed in doing it, as much as I like it and it turned out to be a great album, there were still the same tensions, if I can put it that way. Just underlying tension with Phil and with Michael, who was just as crazy as ever. I had done so much in those ten years that I hadn't seen them. I had done so much of my life, and these guys, man, they haven't moved on. They're still arguing about the same shit. The biggest thing for me was Michael still didn't seem very stable, I think is the best word I can use. They wanted me to go to tour with them."

"So here's the deal, and this is mostly Michael: 'I don't want to get a record company involved. They're just going to rip us off. We're just going to press up the CDs and we're going to take them on the road and sell them at the gig.' I thought man, you know what? It was decision time for me. I've got this good-for-life job, with a car, pension, medical benefits, all this kind of stuff waiting for me in England, or I've got UFO again, with Michael and Phil. I said to my wife, 'Honey, I just can't see this lasting. I just don't think I want to do this. Just chuck everything in and do this.' So basically I got out, and it became, 'The album's great, guys, but I'm not going to do the tour.'"

But the deal toward the making of the record was acceptable financially, says Andy. "Well, yes, we got paid. We got the money up front from the Japanese record company. They only wanted Japan and Asia. They said you can do what you like with it everywhere else. So at that point, we just had the money up front, and made the record, and had this big advance. But I'm telling you honestly, the record company sold the record in Japan, but Michael didn't want to do a deal with an American record label. He didn't want to do a deal with anybody else. He just wanted to sell the record himself and I thought that was crazy."

Walk on Water is also the point where Michael negotiates for 50% of the UFO name. Explains Schenker, "I said to them, 'The only way I'm going to join this band, is by giving me 50% of the name of UFO, so that Phil cannot tour this band without me and do all this damage.' So he agreed to that and some other things we disagreed on, and so that was the new plan. We went ahead with this, and like I said, we just kept it going on and off for a while."

But a great UFO record fell out of this soon to fall out marriage, *Walk on Water* brims with personality. The record spits fire with licks, riffs, rhythms and lyrics. Ron Nevison indeed returned to the fold as the band's producer. What's more, the band that would make the record—Mogg, Schenker, Raymond, Way and Parker—represented fully and completely the top line-up the band ever had: these were the five guys that crafted both *Lights Out* and *Obsession*—six, if we included Nevison—as well as the band that rocked us hard all over *Strangers in the Night.*

Walk on Water, recorded at Rumbo Recorders in Canoga Park, California and issued April 14, 1995 by Zero Corporation, kicks off strong with the tall, cool riffing of "A Self Made Man," a track made even better by its unexpected reggae-like break, not to mention Michael's lyrical soloing and a careening heavy metal close—UFO were back in business.

"I really like 'Venus,'" says Michael, focussing on track two as a particularly fond memory. "*Walk on Water* was a great album—the perfect continuation after *Strangers in the Night*. Again, for me, each song, I'm writing most of the songs and each song comes from the well within and there is a reason for the songs to be there, as far as I'm concerned. So I look at it differently, but I never really listen back to my music. I keep on moving. So it's a bit hard for me to go back there and connect. Because I do my thing from such a deep level, it takes a long time for me to get back to that same place I was when I did it. I don't have any reason to do that, really, because I've done it and it's recorded and it's there for people to enjoy. I'm a creator, so I go on with the next."

Poppy yet proud and pomp-rocking, "Venus" rocks melodically at the open, repeated for the chorus, but drops out to acoustic for the verse. On any of the past three UFO records, events would conspire to sink a song like this, but on *Walk on Water*, there's an authority of delivery that turns every proposal into a winner.

"Pushed to the Limit" was an interesting construct, rhythmically as straight as they come, yet topped with a series of riffs that step out of 4/4 time to resolve themselves, Phil turning in a fiery autobiographical lyric about literally fighting his way out of the clutches of old age and its boring pastimes.

Next up is the album's drop-dead classic, "Stopped by a Bullet (of Love)" being an exquisite pop song, highly strung on acoustic guitar strumming, its electric break riffs intellectually and perfectly fitted to the angelic verse. Phil's lyric circles around the fragmented film noire story crumbs we'll be seeing more of, especially on subsequent albums—both with Michael—*Sharks* and *Covenant*. Still, it's a method that allows Mogg to cover a lot of territory in a short roll of the dice.

"Darker Days" is a stomping, free-burning hard rocker that turns gothic and elegant come Michael's stinging chorus riff. "Running on Empty" is an interesting experiment, nearly an acoustic rockabilly, Phil telling the naughty tale of a married man looking for a little "couch dancer" in the want ads.

"I came in with that," says Pete with respect to the so-Pete "Knock, Knock," a song full up with Stones. "At certain times in my career or whatever, I just want to be a bass player. So I handed that one in; I probably had a couple of other things. It was just an easy song to do. But like I say, sometimes I go into albums just wanting to be a bass player. It's bad enough having to be with the bad boys (laughs), worrying what's going to happen next. When you put four or five members of UFO together around that, it's hard work, but you know what? I think there's a lot of charisma around the hard work. Even though everybody goes, 'Oh, I don't get on with him,' that sort of thing. But I do think there is still magic there." Indeed, "Knock, Knock" is the only *Walk on Water* song not credited to Schenker/Mogg.

Closing this strident, confident record is "Dreaming of Summer," another exquisitely crafted pop song, shimmering with hard rock, but never really going there, like Thin Lizzy at their best, UFO writing a ballad that moves briskly and with a strong back hand.

What's stuck on the end of the record depends on which version of the thing you got. The Japanese Zero Corporation issue of the album includes new versions of "Doctor Doctor" and "Lights Out," with "Doctor Doctor" including some amusing and creatively worthy new licks from Michael (which he interestingly retains for the rendition of the song on his *Unforgiven World Tour* live album from four years later). As well, there's a pointless "Message to Japan." The US fan club issue omits "Message" and "Lights Out" and shuffles the order. The European Eagle issue includes offshoot bonus material: "Fortune Town" from Mogg/Way, "I Will Be There" from MSG and "Public Enemy No.1" from the Paul Raymond Project. The belated 1998 US issue features different cover art and deletes "Message for Japan."

"I like "Darker Days," which is a song we never played live," says Paul Raymond, offering reminiscences on the record. "And I like the Pete Way song, "Knock, Knock," and "Pushed to the Limit" is great; we always played that one live. We should maybe start doing that again. Yeah, that's a great record. I was out of the picture for a lot of it because unfortunately my father passed away during the conception of the album, and I had to go back to England for the funeral and all that stuff. When I got back, they were already recording. So I missed out on a lot of it, to be honest with you."

"Something I didn't like is that we re-recorded "Doctor Doctor" and I don't think we added anything to it—or to "Lights Out." It was just like, what was the point of doing it again? With Ron Nevison as well, which was pointless. But it was a good record, yeah. I liked working with Ron from a keyboard point of view. With Ron, he'd really kick your ass and he would make you work. 'Come on, you've got to find something for this!' He was good like that, a good, hard taskmaster. A lot of people like the Hammond organ stuff that I've done. They say, we don't hear enough of that on the new record (this chat was conducted during the *You Are Here* tour). Well, it's the producer. He didn't think it was necessary. So maybe I should have been a bit more forthright at times. But yes, that Hammond sound, it's on "Pushed to the Limit" and it's there on all that *Walk on Water* stuff. Just hanging in there; it's a nice texture. Hammond is a great instrument. You can't beat it."

But as alluded to, it all went bad out on the road. In the fall of '95, a show had to be cancelled in Modesto, California, where at 9:30, 10:00, with a full house, the promoter was informed that Michael thought he had the day off and was 150 miles away. Shortly thereafter, Sacramento and Nevada also were cancelled at the last minute, due to no-shows from Michael.

"I think the most disappointing point was when we got back together in 1995," says Phil, looking back. "I had high expectations that we were going to really put the effort into doing something and that all went pear-shaped. As far as that went I kept completely out of it; we had our own manager and he had his own manager. I had nothing to say; all I wanted to do was show up, sing and write and play, that's all. I had no opinion. I felt I'd see how that goes and look what happened: he left the band three times then. Modesto, and there was Tokyo where he walked off in the middle of the show which was unbelievable because the audience was just standing in silence; and finally Manchester."

"It isn't bad eggs or anything but what conclusion do you draw from it? Michael has a reputation for doing this. A band can't carry on like that when all you want to do is just go on and play. All the rest of it, that was him coming and going. He went off and had his own career with Chrysalis anyways with MSG, but I was very disappointed when we got back together in 1995 because I thought we were really going to put the effort into it. We once got on very well; we did a lot of stuff together and we had a good thing going there, but people change. The honeymoon was over; it would be like going back to save a failed marriage. It just ain't working (laughs). For me I try to forget all that. I think the guy is a great player and has tremendous potential and I enjoyed playing with him. It's just a shame about all this crap; I think it's all shit, who did what or who said that—it doesn't matter. It's basically you do it and go out and play or you don't. Shut up or ship out."

As mentioned, Andy would be gone, and unlike Michael, not back for *Covenant* and *Sharks*. As Andy explains, "I was thinking, what happens if Michael's had enough two weeks into the tour? What the fuck happens to me? So I just decided that was it. Now, I went back to England, went about my business, and it was months later that my wife happened to be on the Internet and saw something, and what they have done is, they actually sold the album to a European company, and gone off and got a large advance from the record company in Europe, and they'd gone off on tour, and... disaster. This is the time when Michael just kept disappearing off the tour. I think it happened in Europe, America, three or four times, so I felt justified in my decision."

"But as it turned out, they had this money from this record company in Europe and they hadn't given me my share (laughs). So I went to see the record company when I found out. Which didn't go down very well with the guys in the band. It was like, nothing against them. It's just like hey, you know, I was the fifth person on the album. If you're getting an advance of money on album sales, then a fifth of it's mine and they'd spent it all! They'd done these rehearsals, done this disastrous European tour, and all the money was gone so I had to go back to the record company and they said, 'Well, they already said that you were okay. That you were okay with that.' Well, I'm not. I didn't even know. Basically, I got it in the end. It didn't cost the band anything. The record company just paid up."

"But I like the album," continues Parker. "I don't know about you; I thought it was good. It was interesting; it was done in a slightly different way. Phil and I had this thing about analogue drum kits. Obviously, everyone has gone digital, and I've always felt that drums mostly suffer. So what we did on *Walk on Water* with Ron was we recorded the drums on analogue, and then he just jumped the tracks, jumped his stereo mix off of it, and did everything else digitally. When he mixed the album back, he just linked the two machines together so he had nice clean drum tracks that hadn't been worn out with millions of overdubs. Which is what used to happen in the old days. The tape went through the machine so many times—putting the lyrics down, putting Michael's solos down, bass overdubs, stuff like that—they always tended to sound worn-out, the drums."

"Which is why I like the live album too, because you're getting this pristine thing. Unfortunately it's the problem with tape. Every time you put it through the machine, it wears out a little bit. The tape has been through the machine hundreds and hundreds of times. But that didn't happen on *Walk on Water*, because he just stuck the tapes away, and when he mixed down, he brought the fresh drum tracks out and mixed them together. But it takes a lot of equipment and it's an expensive way to do it."

"But yes, having been away from them for ten years, there was this weird tension, like unresolved stuff going on. So when they asked if I would do the tour I just felt that it was destined for trouble. I just had this feeling. I went back to England to work for my family and so for 11-and-a-half years I didn't play drums virtually at all. Once in a while I would play with some friends of mine, just covers and stuff, but basically I was completely out of the business."

So the torch was passed, says Pete, to Simon Wright. "Andy didn't want to work with Michael, because he didn't know what was going to happen next, because of cancelled shows, Michael being in a good mood or a bad mood. Michael liked working with Andy, but Andy decided that he didn't really want to tour; he didn't want the stress of it. He got himself involved in his family company, they had asked him to and he wanted to leave America, because he was getting divorced as well. It wasn't very difficult to change from Andy to Simon; Andy plays slightly different but Simon certainly puts in a good show."

The problems with Michael ultimately led to the band hiring Vinnie Moore, who has had now a fifteen-year run with the band. But first there was a dalliance with Europe guitarist John Norum.

"Because of consistent problems with Michael," says Pete, "we wanted to continue as a band. John was a friend; he's come to a lot of shows and been in contact and of course he's a very good player. There was a possibility, but then Europe reformed, so that went out of the question. We'd been recommended that Vinnie might be really good, but we were a bit worried because of Vinnie's reputation for playing really fast and didn't know if it would be right. We sent some ideas over for songs and you know, Vinnie can play in any style and we bonded very well. With John, we didn't actually play together, but only because we were in different countries. We never made arrangements to get together. It was always a possibility, but when the Europe situation became possible, it was better for him to do that than to see how it would go with UFO."

"Regarding Michael, you've heard the stories from the tour," opines

Tonka from the sidelines, watching the band implode. "I think a large part of it is ego and resentment. I think there's a bit of that 'water takes the path of least resistance' idea. It's easy to be UFO. There is nothing else going on at the time so you do it. The path of least opposition is always the easiest."

Also during this drama-filled era for the band, Michael, improbably, began a string of solid MSG records, beginning with *Written in the Sand* in August of '96. Meanwhile, now that UFO couldn't operate as such without Schenker, Phil and Pete wound up with the stodgy *Edge of the World* record, released June 24, 1997, under the silly moniker of Mogg/Way (guitarist George Bellas and drummer Aynsley Dunbar were also part of the brew). This was hot on the heels of a strange Schenker retrospective issued the previous month called *The Michael Schenker Story Live*.

As the years ground on, and after duct-taping the band back together yet again—Michael included (and Simon Wright on drums)—UFO toured Europe with Danger Danger and the UK with Dirty Deeds. This was in early '98, in support of the now quite aged *Walk on Water*, which was just now seeing European and (proper) US issue. However over in Japan a fight ensued and Michael walked off, only three days into that leg of the tour. Michael proceeded to take MSG on Europe's version of the G3 tour, accompanying Joe Satriani and Uli Jon Roth.

In February '99, Michael launched yet another very nice MSG record in *The Unforgiven*. Said Sir Schenker, "Well it's a different singer; different musicians make a difference. It's a different singer, a different bass player, a different producer, different studio, different year, and all of these things make a difference."

Offered Michael upon working with Shrapnel Records head Mike Varney for the first time, "Over the years he's called me up to do things with me and we never got together. He did a project with Mogg/Way and there was a song that I thought was very well-produced, and I knew there was definitely a possibility to do something with Mike. When I finished the G3 tour in Europe with Joe Satriani, I decided to make a new album, and the first thing I had to take care of was the producer situation. So I called Mike up and he immediately suggested Kelly Keeling as the singer, and he sent a tape and there were a couple of songs where I liked the vocals very much. So I told Mike to make sure that he was going to sing on that level, and not scream so much. He also suggested the bass player John Onder, and that was it. Shane Gaalaas and Seth Bernstein were already in the band and that was basically it."

"It was just something to do with the UFO tour we did," says Michael cryptically about the title of the record. "We had to cancel a few shows in Japan because I was sick. We were basically in a funny way; it felt funny. I wanted to redo the concerts at a later date and nobody was interested, and everybody was just blaming me and this and that, and the promoter wanted his money. So I just felt like I was considered as this unforgiving type of a person. It was like, 'You got sick and that's it; we don't want anything to do with this person.' It was a weird situation."

Said Michael further on the subject of his break with UFO, "We got together because we thought we had a great manager, but being on the road and going through certain experiences, I found he wasn't the right person at all. Instances like, we would get together for a tour and I didn't know which plane to take, I didn't know which hotel we were staying in, I didn't know what rehearsal room it was, stuff like that. I can't waste my time with that. I think UFO needs somebody with heart and soul, not someone that just opens his hand for money, but somebody who really works his butt off in small details as well as the big picture. So when that person shows up, there is a future for UFO with me involved, but until then, I can't waste my time with it. We need management who is very organized in order to make it work. So, there is a possibility that UFO will reunite again, given the proper management and direction. If everything seems right and everyone says yes."

"I had been with UFO over the years because of music," mused Michael, in a separate interview, "not because I had such a great relationship with the people. It's a musical relationship basically, and with UFO, nothing can happen until they find management that is there with heart and soul, and I think UFO in general deserves better. So if this person ever turns up, maybe there's a future for UFO."

In that same 1999 chat, Michael goes on to explain that he had broken off relations with the infamous Bela Piper ("She does some wholesale from a different location, and she gets a percentage, but that's about it."), and that plans to move to Hawaii and build a studio complex there were also off.

The Unforgiven was followed up later the same year with a double live CD called (at least on the spine – yeesh!) *Unforgiven World Tour*, which included eight UFO classics among the album's twenty-one tracks, as well as a run through Scorpions' speed metal scorcher "Another Piece of Meat." Also in '99, UFO alumnus Tommy McClendon returned alongside Tesla's Brian Wheat on CMC International with a self-titled modern metal album under the moniker Soulmotor.

Meanwhile, on September 21, 1999, Mogg/Way hatched their second plot, the incredible *Chocolate Box* album, possibly the second greatest record to come out of the immediate orbit around the band proper, after MSG's *Assault Attack*.

Given that *Chocolate Box* featured Phil, Pete, Paul Raymond and even satellite UFO member Simon Wright, I asked the guitarist for the record (and future $ign of Four member with Phil), Jeff Kollman, if he ever saw Phil trying to tug the UFO brand name back from Michael and call this great record what it arguably could be comfortably packaged as—a hugely impressive UFO record, new guitarist to be sure, but one who plays like an intensely creative and energetic Michael Schenker.

"No, he didn't think he had a chance to do that," explains Jeff. "To be honest with you, I think for the longest time he figured there was no way Michael would ever give it back to him. Finally he got so fed up, he just asked him, and he said yeah. They had signed an agreement, I think when they did *Walk on Water*, that they couldn't be UFO without each other. But they had so much turmoil and I think Michael finally had a momentary lapse of common sense (laughs), and realised that they don't work together, they just don't. Musically they do, but personality-wise, Michael is a beast all on his own."

"Mike Varney actually referred me to him," furthers Kollman, on meeting Phil for the first time. "It was funny, because it was a week after I played with Michael on the European tour. I played with Michael in '98, on the G3 tour and I got along with Michael great. I had no problems with him or anything. But he's so complicated a character. I personally don't have any problems with him, but I've just heard—and sort of seen—so much. The last thing I know is that he bought a moped and put a guitar on his back and drove to Mexico and ended up in a jail (laughs). But I think a week after that tour, Mike Varney called me, or Phil called me directly, and said he was looking for a guitar player. Then I just wrote a few songs in my studio, and got together and played them for him and he said, 'Yeah, that's it.' "Last Man in Space" was one of them and then, let's see, I would think "Muddy's Gold" was the other one. And that pretty much clinched it. I love working with Phil. I don't know how much time between records or what the name of the band will be called, but I have a feeling I'll always be doing stuff with him."

Digging into this powerful, classy album, Kollman says that "Jerusalem" and "Muddy's Gold" are personal favourites. Also, "there are a couple Pete Way songs that I really like. He wrote two particularly, "Sparkling Wine" and "Death in the Family." Actually in my band, I do "Jerusalem" live. I'd much rather have Phil up there singing it. Now, my writing is not all that different, because I wrote the music for 90% of that record. So when you hear my stuff, it's not all that different. The Mogg/Way is going to sound a little more like classic rock and mine is going to sound a little newer and edgier. But it's not that much of a departure, because when I write, I write what I like. My music isn't all that different. It's coming from the same place."

Made much like the present-day UFO album it is, Kollman says, "We all got together up at Mike Varney's place. I had four or five or six songs I already had basic ideas for. I did some pre-production with the drummer that I was staying with at the time, Shane Gaalaas. I think we were up at Mike Varney's place for a good ten days, Prairie Sun Studios, and we just all jammed out together. Paul Raymond was there; it was a whole band thing. Pete was great. He's a character; I love Pete. I haven't seen Paul since back then, but man, we got along great. Paul is a great, great musician, great to hang with. We'd drink a little wine here and there (laughs), a little civilized entertainment."

"Difficult to say really, because there are some good songs on them," answers Pete when asked to contrast *Chocolate Box* with the first Mogg/Way record. "It's like... I wish some of them were UFO songs. When I did those, to be truthful, I had a very bad drug problem. So if you're injecting opiates and heroin and this that and the other— methadone here and there—it's very difficult. I can't say to you which songs... there were some good songs written by me and Phil. I stretched Phil's patience to the limit doing them, if you see what I mean (laughs)."

So would you say the Mogg/Way years were your worst with respect to having a drug problem then? "Difficult to say, because you don't really know you've got one. Know what I mean? I thought it was quite normal to inject drugs. Then going back to a huge cocaine problem after that, from injecting heroin and when my wife died from a cocaine overdose, injecting that, then you go, 'Ooh, maybe I should take this drug thing seriously.' The worst thing I actually find is alcohol. I'm really trying to get rid of my alcohol problem. When I say I have a problem, I probably don't drink more than anybody else. But I like a drink. You know, I question it."

Continues Jeff, sticking to the discreet road, "The interesting thing with those guys is that I was coming in with all these songs and all these ideas. Then it's going Phil and I, because he's the singer and I'm the main contribution to the music. Paul saw that there was a chemistry there, and he was like… if he should have a rock star ego, he didn't, and he would just put it aside and go, 'okay, my job here is try to support what's happening here.' These guys wouldn't come in and go, 'Hey, I'm Paul Raymond, and get out of the way while I write this song or do this.' It wasn't anything like that. Everybody was just trying to contribute to the ideas that Phil and I had."

"He always adds stuff," says Kollman, characterizing Mike Varney, an important figure now in UFO folklore. "He's good at arranging things and keeping everybody together and he's a very musical guy. So Mike always has a lot of musical contribution. He always reminds us of the essence of UFO, and where we draw the line, as far as sounding too much alike or drifting too far away. Certainly a song like "Last Man in Space," that guitar riff, that's definitely like "Mother Mary" and the essence of UFO. A little bit of that was great. So he was a good producer for that. He allowed me a lot of freedom to help mix the record and really took a lot of care to the end."

"Oh yeah, Simon, he's got all kinds of chops," offers Kollman on *Chocolate Box*'s drummer Simon Wright, also of AC/DC and Dio fame, essentially a guy not known for busy playing. "But I think what moves him is just to play four on the floor and a really fat groove. Because at the end of the day, all that matters is the groove. You can play all the chops in the world, but it's never about that. Bonham, all his chops for "Moby Dick" and all that never really mattered. It's just his groove. Simon comes from that school, the Bonham school, where it's just a fat groove, laid back snare, four on the floor, and it feels great. Drummers who have a lot of chops, if they're smart, they end up getting back to that. I work with Shane Gaalaas who I think is one of the greatest drummers in the world. He has more chops than anybody on the frickin' planet, but now he's going back to just, 'I've got to make my groove feel better.' Analysing it."

In agreement with other insider characterizations of Phil's lyrics, Kollman remarks that "Phil is a character. Sometimes, he'll come up with a lyric… there's something off of $ign of Four, like "Cold Cactus Blue." Okay, what does that mean? I think sometimes he just carries around phrases. Like, 'I like the way that sounds. I'm not sure what it's supposed to mean in the grand scheme, but it feels cool.' He's really like that. Or I'll think it doesn't mean much, and I'll look at it later and I'll go, 'Wow, that's pretty genius.' I think he's one of the genius storytellers, and he's always pretty quick, actually. I think quicker with *Chocolate*

Box than he was with $ign of Four. I think he took a little bit more time and care for $ign of Four. Not that it came out better or anything, but he had the luxury. Usually when Mike Varney is involved, things tend to have to go at a breakneck speed, so you'd better hang on tight, and hope it comes out great."

With regard to Phil's vocals... "He's got such an endearing quality to his voice. He's completely opposite to another gentleman I've worked with, which is Glenn Hughes, a lot lately. I've worked with Glenn and produced a couple of records for him in the past two years and Glenn's vocal chops galore. He can just rely on his ability to sing stuff that nobody else can sing. Whereas Phil is a completely different type of singer. It's more of an endearing quality and the way he delivers a lyric, more so than the singer's singer with the chops. Somehow, that really lasts. You never get sick of his voice, because he's not in your face. I mean, I get sick of Chris Cornell after seven songs on a record, and he's one of the most brilliant singers there is. Because there's so much of him; he's filling up so much space and there are so many ranges. Whereas Phil is so subtle, and great things are always of a subtle nature."

After seeing Phil in such top physical form on the *You Are Here* tour, I asked Jeff if he ever saw Phil in any sort of serious workout regimen. "He must work out at home," laughs Kollman. "When he's out here, he's pretty much relaxing and writing. But yeah, I've heard he's looking good. He must have a good regimen when he's at home. I don't see him eat. Salad in the morning and a couple of beers at night (laughs)."

Epilogue

"The last few years have been tough"

A nd thus we conclude the second instalment documenting various UFO sightings, spanning two decades, the '80s and the '90s.

But it sure as heck has ended on a high note, hasn't it? *Walk on Water* was a fine, fine UFO album, a victory lap, really (he says, drinking gin and listening to "Stopped by a Bullet (of Love)"). But hot on the heels, stealth-like—and not to be forgotten if I can help it—is Mogg/Way's *Chocolate Box*, like I say, easily way more of a UFO album than, say, *Misdemeanour*, *Ain't Misbehavin'* and *High Stakes & Dangerous Men*.

Chocolate Box... I suppose the message there is, if we read between the lines, this is UFO screwing up, not knowing what they have, in this case, not knowing what they have in Jeff Kollman. Indeed, not continuing with that line-up can be chalked up to just another one in a line of endless career mishaps.

This is an epilogue, so we should take care of business. The rest of the story in summary (for maybe there will be a third instalment in this series—who doesn't like the word trilogy?) goes something like this.

Quite surprisingly, UFO would enter the 2000s cranking out two records with Michael Schenker as the band's guitarist, namely, 2000's *Covenant* and 2002's *Sharks*. After that, the band would bring in American Vinnie Moore to fill the all-important axe spot, and little did anybody know, but Vinnie would turn out to be permanent.

You Are Here, issued 2004, would feature Phil, Paul, Pete and Vinnie, along with drummer Jason Bonham. *The Monkey Puzzle*, issued in 2006, would find Andy Parker returning to the fold. The band would hit delete on Pete for 2009's *The Visitor*, officially presenting themselves as a four-piece, evoking memories of the

Making Contact album a quarter-century earlier. *Seven Deadly* would follow in 2012, bass slot still essentially not resolved, with 2015's *A Conspiracy of Stars* ushering in the talented and dependable Rob de Luca into the bass position.

This is the line-up that would record 2017's *The Salentino Cuts*, a crap covers album, a record that unfortunately looks to serve as the band's last. Post-release, there has been talk from Phil of retirement after the band's 2019 tour dates. An official press release, entitled "A Statement from Phil Mogg," reads as follows:

"Phil Mogg has confirmed that next year's 50th anniversary tour with UFO will be his last as the front man of the long-running hard rock band. Consequently, it seems almost certain that at that point they will cease to exist. UFO were formed in London in 1969 and Mogg is their only ever-present member, performing on all of the group's twenty-two studio albums. 'This decision has been a long time coming; I've considered stepping down at the end of UFO's previous two tours,' Mogg explains. 'I don't want to call this a farewell tour as I hate that word, but next year's gigs will represent my final tap-dancing appearances with the band.'"

"'2019 marks UFO's 50th anniversary, so the timing feels right,' he continues. 'There will be a final tour of the UK and we will also play some shows in selected other cities that the band has a strong connection with. But outside of the UK this won't be a long tour. Being out on the road isn't always tremendously luxurious and although the playing is as great as it ever was, the stuff that surrounds it becomes very tiresome. I always told myself that when I reached that stage I would step down, and that's what I'm going to do. This is the right time for me to quit.'"

"Mogg turned 70 in April 2018 and although his voice remains strong, he admits that age played its part in his conclusion. 'I'm a big reader of obituaries, and my finger always goes down to: "I wonder how old they were...",' he chuckles. 'The last few years have been tough; losing Lemmy was awful and I was sad that Jimmy Bain passed on a cruise ship. That distressed me quite a lot.'"

"While many veteran bands in such a position simply cease playing live and continue to record, UFO will no longer be releasing new music. Last year's covers collection, *The Salentino Cuts*, is set to become a signing-off point, though Mogg insists that however unlikely the prospect might seem—the singer is a lone strand of consistency throughout a fifty-year history—he would have no problem with UFO continuing with a replacement. The band's current line-up—completed by keyboard player/second guitarist Paul Raymond, guitarist Vinnie Moore, drummer Andy Parker and bassist Rob De Luca—have of course been informed of Mogg's decision. 'I've told the guys that this is how it is,' he says. 'They know it's my time to go and they know that they can do whatever they want to do without me but I don't want to play live or make records any more, though having said that I might go on and do an album of my own. I'll have to see how I feel about that.'"

"Of course UFO have either split up, retired or gone on hiatus several times before, but Mogg is keen to make the distinction that next year's dates don't just mark the end of his touring commitments with UFO—for Phil, there will be no further concerts of any kind."

"'For me, this is the end of my stint with UFO,' he clarifies. 'This is a line in the sand. I'm suggesting we call the tour Last Orders, though I also like The Bar Is Closing. I'm also tempted to name it The Drinks Are on Parker,' he chuckles, referring to long-suffering sticksman Andy Parker."

"You'll have gathered that Mogg is not about to slash his wrists anytime soon. Of course he is sad that the finishing line is now within sight but he has had sufficient time to live with and process such a massive personal decision. 'Maybe the best word to use is bittersweet,' he concludes. 'But my time has arrived and all that remains is to make sure that we have a good tour.'"

Discography

A. 1980 - 1999

Note: this is primarily a UK discography, i.e. discography of "first issue," given that UFO are a British band. UK issue is used for spellings and punctuation of song titles, timings and credits. I've used the notes section as a sort of free-form area to bring up limited additional points I considered salient. Personnel is only addressed at the outset and then when a change is made. This is the only place songs aren't in double quote marks (or single, when toggled inside of speaker quotations). Side 1/Side 2 designation is maintained for albums issued in the vinyl era and then put aside at the rise of the CD age, basically 1990.

No Place to Run
(Chrysalis CDL 1239, January '80)
Side 1: 1. Alpha Centauri (Chapman) 1:57; 2. Lettin' Go (Chapman, Way, Mogg) 3:58; 3. Mystery Train (Parker, Phillips) 3:54; 4. This Fire Burns Tonight (Chapman, Mogg) 4:13; 5. Gone in the Night (Chapman, Mogg) 3:43
Side 2: 1. Youngblood (Way, Mogg) 3:57; 2. No Place to Run (Chapman, Mogg) 3:58; 3. Take It of Leave It (Raymond) 2:58; 4. Money, Money (Way, Mogg) 3:25; 5. Anyday (Chapman, Mogg) 3:48
Notes: Slight variations in colours used for cover typography across territories. Personnel: Phil Mogg – vocals; Paul Chapman – guitars; Paul Raymond – keyboards, guitars, vocals; Pete Way – bass; Andy Parker – drums.

The Wild, the Willing and the Innocent
(Chrysalis CHR 1307, January '81)
Side 1: 1. Chains, Chains (Way, Mogg) 3:24; 2. Long Gone (Chapman, Mogg) 5:18; 3. The Wild, the Willing and the Innocent (Chapman, Mogg) 4:58; 5. It's Killing Time (Way, Mogg) 4:30
Side 2: 1. Makin' Moves (Chapman, Mogg) 4:45; 2. Lonely Heart (Chapman, Way, Mogg) 5:08; 3. Couldn't Get It Right (Chapman, Way, Mogg) 4:32; 5. Profession of Violence (Chapman, Mogg) 4:20
Notes: Neil Carter replaces Paul Raymond, curiously maintaining same credit: keyboards, guitar and vocals. Like its predecessor, slight variants, depending on territory, exist in the cover art, with the type and with the photography. Strictly speaking, "Makin' Moves" is "Makin Moves," both on the back cover and the record label, but throughout the book I've gone with the more grammatically correct "Makin' Moves."

Mechanix

(Chrysalis CHR 1360, February '82)

Side 1: 1. The Writer (Chapman, Mogg, Carter) 4:10; 2. Somethin' Else (Cochran, Sheeley) 3:20; 3. Back into My Life (Way, Mogg) 4:56; 4. You'll Get Love (Chapman, Carter, Mogg) 3:10; 5. Doing It All for You (Way, Chapman, Carter, Mogg) 5:00
Side 2: 1. We Belong to the Night (Way, Carter, Mogg) 3:55; 2. Let It Rain (Way, Carter, Mogg) 4:01; 3. Terri (Chapman, Mogg) 3:50; 4. Feel It (Way, Mogg) 4:05; 5. Dreaming (Carter, Mogg) 3:56

Making Contact

(Chrysalis CHR 1402, February '83)

Side 1: 1. Blinded by a Lie (Carter, Mogg) 4:03; 2. Diesel in the Dust (Carter, Mogg) 4:22; 3. A Fool for Love (Carter, Mogg) 3:53; 4. You and Me (Carter, Mogg) 3:27; 5. When It's Time to Rock (Chapman, Mogg) 5:18
Side 2: 1. The Way the Wild Wind Blows (Chapman, Carter, Mogg) 4:11; 2. Call My Name (Carter, Mogg) 3:12; 3. All Over You (Carter, Mogg) 4:12; 4. No Getaway (Chapman, Carter, Mogg) 3:26; 5. Push, It's Love (Carter, Mogg) 3:10
Notes: Pete Way is no longer with the band; bass duties are split between Paul Chapman and Neil Carter.

Misdemeanor

(Chrysalis CHR 1518, November '85)

Side 1: 1. This Time (Gray, Mogg) 4:39; 2. One Heart (Gray, Mogg, McClendon) 4:22; 3. Night Run (Gray, Mogg, McClendon) 4:23; 4. The Only Ones (Gray, Mogg) 5:16; 5. Meanstreets (McClendon, Mogg) 4:16
Side 2: 1. Heaven's Gate (McClendon, Mogg) 4:14; 2. Blue (Gray, Mogg) 5:07; 3. Dream the Dream (Raymond, Mogg) 4:30; 4. Name of Love (McClendon, Mogg) 4:02; 5. Wreckless (McClendon, Mogg) 4:54
Notes: Only Phil Mogg remains from the previous band line-up. Personnel: Phil Mogg – vocals; Tommy "Atomic Tommy M" McClendon – guitars; Paul Raymond – keyboards, guitars; Paul Gray – bass; Jim Simpson – drums. Slight cover art variants exist, mostly around the prominence of the photo.

Ain't Misbehavin'

(FM WKFMLP 107, February '88)

Side 1: 1. Between a Rock and a Hard Place (McClendon, Mogg) 3:37; 2. Another Saturday Night (Gray, Mogg) 4:39; 3. At War with the World (McClendon, Mogg) 3:03
Side 2: 2. Hunger in the Night (McClendon, Mogg, Gray) 4:10; 2. Easy Money (McClendon, Mogg) 3:37; 3. Rock Boyz, Rock (McClendon, Mogg, Gray, Simpson) 3:19
Notes: Six-track EP of all new original material. Paul Raymond no longer with the band, so UFO at this point is a four-piece. Atomic Tommy M is now Atomik Tommy M.

High Stakes & Dangerous Men

(Essential ESSCD 178, February '92)

1. Borderline (Way, Mogg) 5:18; 2. Primed for One (Archer, Mogg) 3:22; 3. She's the One (Archer, Mogg) 3:45; 4. Ain't Life Sweet (Mogg, Way, Archer, Edwards) 3:42; 5. Don't Want to Lose You (Way, Mogg) 6. Burnin' Fire (Way, Mogg) 4:02; 7. Running Up the Highway (Way, Mogg) 4:40; 8. Back Door Man (Archer, Mogg) 5:08; 9. One of Those Nights (Way, Mogg, Archer) 4:11; 10. Revolution (Way, Mogg) 4:07; 11. Love Deadly Love (Way, Mogg) 4:52; 12. Let the Good Time Roll (Way, Mogg) 4:13
Notes: Only Phil Mogg remains from the previous band line-up. Personnel: Phil Mogg – vocals; Laurence Archer – guitars, backing vocals; Pete Way – bass; Clive Edwards – drums.

Walk on Water

(Zero Corporation XRCN-1237; April '95)

1. A Self Made Man (Schenker, Mogg) 6:24; 2. Venus (Schenker, Mogg) 5:20; 3. Pushed to the Limit (Schenker, Mogg) 3:50; 4. Stopped by a Bullet (of Love) (Schenker, Mogg) 4:35; 5. Darker Days (Schenker, Mogg) 5:37; 6. Running on Empty (Schenker, Mogg) 5:11; 7. Knock, Knock (Way, Mogg)

4:21; 8. Dreaming of Summer (Schenker, Mogg) 7:03; 9. Doctor Doctor '95 (Schenker, Mogg) 4:27; 10. Lights Out '95 (Schenker, Way, Parker, Mogg) 5:13; 11. Message for Japan (UFO) 6:09

Notes: Issued first in Japan and the US (low key); issued in Europe in 1997 and more widespread in the US in 1998 on CMC International Records. Many cover variants exist, along with slight track list variants. Official first issue would be the Japanese release on Zero, given that the project was financed in Japan. Personnel: Phil Mogg – vocals; Michael Schenker – guitars; Paul Raymond – keyboards, guitars, vocals; Pete Way – bass; Andy Parker – drums. This is the line-up last in place for *Lights Out* and *Obsession*.

B. Pre-1980 and post-1999 Summary Discography

Note: As food for thought, and as a quick reference, I thought I'd offer an abbreviated, less-detailed discography of UFO's studio albums produced before and after the period covered in this book. Of course many compilation, live albums and DVDs also saw issue, but I'm drawing the line at this perfunctory checklist of the songs in their original state, so to speak.

UFO Discography: 1970 – 1979

UFO (1970)
UFO 2: Flying (1971)
Phenomenon (1974)
Force It (1975)
No Heavy Petting (1976)
Lights Out (1977)
Obsession (1978)

UFO Discography: 2000 – 2018

Covenant (2000)
Sharks (2002)
You Are Here (2004)
The Monkey Puzzle (2006)
The Visitor (2009)
Seven Deadly (2012)
A Conspiracy of Stars (2015)
The Salentino Cuts (2017)

Credits

A. Interviews with the Author

Laurence Archer: 2009.
Gary Barden: August 19, 2004.
Graham Bonnet: November 28, 2003, January 31, 2005, October 11, 2009, March 27, 2011, June 2018.
Neil Carter: December 10, 2004.
Paul Chapman: August 8, 2000, November 21, 2004, May 16, 2007, 2015.
Steve Dawson: 2012.
Clive Edwards: June 13, 2011.
J.J. French: August 26, 1999, 2004.
Paul Gray: November 18, 2017.
Dave King: June 2001.
Jeff Kollman: January 2001, 2004.
Alex Lifeson: October 3, 2003.
Gary Lyons: May 2007.
Leo Lyons: December 6, 2004.
Yngwie Malmsteen: January 18, 2004, September 24, 2008.
Bernie Marsden: April 17, 2002, 2003, June 13, 2013, March 25, 2014.
Robin McAuley: March 4, 2012.
Tommy McClendon: April 15, 2002.
Phil Mogg: September 22, 2000, January 22, 2004, January 30, 2004, October 11, 2013.
Ron Nevison: 2009, March 4, 2011.
Andy Parker: September 25, 2006, March 16, 2007, May 17, 2007, May 5, 2009, February 1, 2012, October 11, 2013, January 15, 2015.
Danny Peyronel: September 29, 2004.
Paul Raymond: 2003, September 27, 2004, February 14, 2013.
Michael Schenker: 1999, December 6, 2001, November 7, 2003, September 23, 2004, March 4, 2012, October 18, 2012, December 20, 2013.
Billy Sheehan: 1998, July 20, 2001, April 18, 2009.
Nick Tauber: June 28, 2011.
Chris Tsangarides: February 17, 2006, 2010.
Pete Way: September 12, 2000, 2002, early 2004, October 3, 2004.
Kit Woolven: 2009.
Graham Wright: October 29, 2004.

Note: If the above seems a little lacking in detail, it's because some of it is a little hazy, entailing backstage areas and tour buses, where various band members drifted in and out of the conversation. In addition to the above interviews with Phil Mogg, on July 30, 1999, I interviewed on the phone... a Phil Mogg imposter! Within ten seconds of talking to the mystery man, I knew it wasn't Phil, but fascinated, I conducted the interview anyway. Before the summer was out, I was told by a reader that on a flight, someone was impersonating me, regaling this reader and his buddy about the writing of all of these rock books. Make of this what you will.

B. Additional Sources

Classic Rock Revisited (www.classicrockrevisited.com).
  Interviews by Jeb Wright, Shelly Harris and Ryan Sparks.
Hit Parader. Flying High by Rob Andrews. 1986. Charlton Publications, Charlton Bldg., Derby, CT 06418
Hit Parader. Waysted Metal Madness by Andy Secher. April 1984.
  Charlton Publications, Charlton Bldg., Derby, CT 06418.
Let It Rock (dmme.net). Interviews with Neil Carter and Phil Mogg by Dmitry M. Epstein.
Metal Hammer. Train Kept a Rollin' by Pippa Lang.
Metal Rules (metal-rules.com). Interviews with Andy Parker and Pete Way by Marko Syrjala.
Misty Green and Blue (strangers-in-the-night.com). Misty Green, Blue and Gray by Kate Batttttty (sic).
Misty Green and Blue (strangers-in-the-night.com). Interview with Pete Way by Mike McCann.
  Issue One 1994.
Raw. High Stakes for the Dangerous Duo! By Kirk Blows, May 13 – 26, 1992, No. 97.
  EMAP Metro, P.O. Box 3AU London UK W1A 3AU.
Record Collector. The UFO Has Landed by Tim Jones, March 2001, No. 259.
  Parker Mead Limited for Parker Publishing, 43/45 St. Mary's Road, Ealing, London W5 5RQ.
Rip. Twenty Years at Warp Speed by Del James, October 1989.
  L.F.P. Inc., 9171 Wilshire Blvd., Suite 300, Beverly Hills, CA 90210.
Rock Scene. UFO On The Horizon by George Sulmers. 1987.
Shockwaves. Interview with Michael Schenker by Bob Nalbandian.

About the Author

At approximately 7900 (with over 7000 appearing in his books), Martin has unofficially written more record reviews than anybody in the history of music writing across all genres. Additionally, Martin has penned over eighty books on hard rock, heavy metal, classic rock and record collecting. He was Editor In Chief of the now retired *Brave Words & Bloody Knuckles*, Canada's foremost metal publication for 14 years, and has also contributed to *Revolver*, *Guitar World*, *Goldmine*, *Record Collector*, bravewords.com, lollipop.com and hardradio.com, with many record label band bios and liner notes to his credit as well. Additionally, Martin has been a regular contractor to Banger Films, having worked for two years as researcher on the award-wining documentary *Rush: Beyond the Lighted Stage*, on the writing and research team for the 11-episode *Metal Evolution* and on the ten-episode *Rock Icons*, both for VH1 Classic. Additionally, Martin is the writer of the original metal genre chart used in *Metal: A Headbanger's Journey* and throughout the *Metal Evolution* episodes. Martin currently resides in Toronto and can be reached through martinp@inforamp.net or www.martinpopoff.com.

Martin Popoff Bibliography

Lights Out: Surviving the '70s with UFO (2018)
AC/DC: Album by Album (2017)
Led Zeppelin: All the Albums, All the Songs (2017)
Tornado of Souls: Thrash's Titanic Clash (2017)
Caught in a Mosh: The Golden Era of Thrash (2017)
Metal Collector: Gathered Tales from Headbangers (2017)
Rush: Album by Album (2017)
Beer Drinkers and Hell Raisers: The Rise of Motörhead (2017)
Hit the Lights: The Birth of Thrash (2017)
Popoff Archive – 4: Classic Rock (2017)
Popoff Archive – 3: Hair Metal (2017)
Popoff Archive – 2: Progressive Rock (2016)
Popoff Archive – 1: Doom Metal (2016)
Rock the Nation: Montrose, Gamma and Ronnie Redefined (2016)
Punk Tees: The Punk Revolution in 125 T-Shirts (2016)
Metal Heart: Aiming High with Accept (2016)
Ramones at 40 (2016)
Time and a Word: The Yes Story (2016)
Kickstart My Heart: A Mötley Crüe Day-by-Day (2015)
This Means War: The Sunset Years of the NWOBHM (2015)
Wheels of Steel: The Explosive Early Years of the NWOBHM (2015)
Swords and Tequila: Riot's Classic First Decade (2015)
Who Invented Heavy Metal? (2015)
Sail Away: Whitesnake's Fantastic Voyage (2015)
Live Magnetic Air: The Unlikely Saga of the Superlative Max Webster (2014)
Steal Away the Night: An Ozzy Osbourne Day-by-Day (2014)
The Big Book of Hair Metal (2014)
Sweating Bullets: The Deth and Rebirth of Megadeth (2014)
    updated and reissued as So Far, So Good... So Megadeth (2017)
Smokin' Valves: A Headbanger's Guide to 900 NWOBHM Records (2014)
The Art of Metal (co-edit with Malcolm Dome; 2013)
2 Minutes to Midnight: An Iron Maiden Day-By-Day (2013)
Metallica: The Complete Illustrated History (2013); update and reissue (2016)
Rush: The Illustrated History (2013); update and reissue (2016)
Ye Olde Metal: 1979 (2013)
Scorpions: Top of the Bill (2013);
    updated and reissued as Wind of Change: The Scorpions Story (2016)
Epic Ted Nugent (2012);
    updated and reissued as Motor City Madhouse: Going Gonzo with Ted Nugent (2017)
Fade to Black: Hard Rock Cover Art of the Vinyl Age (2012)
It's Getting Dangerous: Thin Lizzy 81-12 (2012)

We Will Be Strong: Thin Lizzy 76-81 (2012)
Fighting My Way Back: Thin Lizzy 69-76 (2011);
     updated and reissued as From Dublin to Jailbreak: Thin Lizzy 1969-76 (2016)
The Deep Purple Royal Family: Chain of Events '80 – '11 (2011)
The Deep Purple Royal Family: Chain of Events Through '79 (2011);
     reissued as The Deep Purple Family Year by Year (to 1979) (2016)
Black Sabbath FAQ (2011)
The Collector's Guide to Heavy Metal: Volume 4: The '00s (2011; co-authored with David Perri)
Goldmine Standard Catalog of American Records 1948 – 1991, 7th Edition (2010)
Goldmine Record Album Price Guide, 6th Edition (2009)
Goldmine 45 RPM Price Guide, 7th Edition (2009)
A Castle Full of Rascals: Deep Purple '83 – '09 (2009)
Worlds Away: Voivod and the Art of Michel Langevin (2009)
Ye Olde Metal: 1978 (2009)
Gettin' Tighter: Deep Purple '68 – '76 (2008)
All Access: The Art of the Backstage Pass (2008)
Ye Olde Metal: 1977 (2008)
Ye Olde Metal: 1976 (2008)
Judas Priest: Heavy Metal Painkillers (2007)
Ye Olde Metal: 1973 to 1975 (2007)
The Collector's Guide to Heavy Metal: Volume 3: The Nineties (2007)
Ye Olde Metal: 1968 to 1972 (2007)
Run For Cover: The Art of Derek Riggs (2006)
Black Sabbath: Doom Let Loose (2006)
Dio: Light Beyond the Black (2006)
The Collector's Guide to Heavy Metal: Volume 2: The Eighties (2005)
Rainbow: English Castle Magic (2005)
UFO: Shoot Out the Lights (2005)
The New Wave of British Heavy Metal Singles (2005)
Blue Öyster Cult: Secrets Revealed! (2004); update and reissue (2009);
     updated and reissued as Agents of Fortune: The Blue Öyster Cult Story (2016)
Contents Under Pressure: 30 Years of Rush at Home & Away (2004)
The Top 500 Heavy Metal Albums of All Time (2004)
The Collector's Guide to Heavy Metal: Volume 1: The Seventies (2003)
The Top 500 Heavy Metal Songs of All Time (2003)
Southern Rock Review (2001)
Heavy Metal: 20th Century Rock and Roll (2000)
The Goldmine Price Guide to Heavy Metal Records (2000)
The Collector's Guide to Heavy Metal (1997)
Riff Kills Man! 25 Years of Recorded Hard Rock & Heavy Metal (1993)

See martinpopoff.com for complete details and ordering information.

Martin Popoff titles available from Wymer Publishing:

From Dublin To Jailbreak
Thin Lizzy 1969-76
Martin Popoff

ISBN: 978-1-908724-39-7
Hardback: 256pp,
1 x 8 b/w plate section
RRP: £19.99

Wind Of Change
The Scorpions Story
Martin Popoff

ISBN: 978-1-908724-40-3
Paperback: 256pp,
1 x 8 b/w plate section
RRP: £14.99

Agents Of Fortune
The Blue Öyster Cult Story
Martin Popoff

ISBN: 978-1-908724-41-0
Paperback: 256pp,
1 x 8 b/w plate section
RRP: £14.99

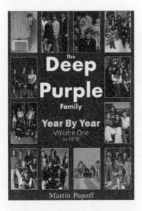

The Deep Purple Family:
Year by Year Vol 1 (- 1979)
Martin Popoff

ISBN: 978-1-908724-42-7
Paperback: 256pp,
Illustrated throughout.
RRP: £14.99

Motor City Madhouse
Going Gonzo with Ted
Nugent
Martin Popoff

ISBN: 978-1-908724-59-5
Paperback: 256pp,
1 x 8 b/w plate section
RRP: £14.99

So Far, So Good...
So Megadeth!
Martin Popoff

ISBN: 978-1-908724-61-8
Paperback: 288pp
RRP: £14.99